Mel Bay Presents

The Guitar Gymnasium

A Mental and Physical Workout, Designed to Develop Flawless Technique

by Robin Hill

MEL BAY

© 2001 BY MEL BAY PUBLICATIONS, INC., PACIFIC, MO 63069.
ALL RIGHTS RESERVED. INTERNATIONAL COPYRIGHT SECURED. B.M.I. MADE AND PRINTED IN U.S.A.
No part of this publication may be reproduced in whole or in part, or stored in a retrieval system, or transmitted in any form
or by any means, electronic, mechanical, photocopy, recording, or otherwise, without written permission of the publisher.

Visit us on the Web at www.melbay.com — E-mail us at email@melbay.com

THE
GUITAR GYMNASIUM
Foreword

Although entitled 'Guitar Gymnasium' this book deals not only with the technical aspects of guitar technique, but also with the many psychological factors inherent in the performance of music on the classical guitar.

It contains many helpful quotations, by musicians and thinkers of the past and present, which I have collected and found inspiring and useful over the years.

Most of *my* thinking on these matters has been precipitated by the 'front line' experiences of concertising, recording, broadcasting and teaching. These practical experiences help to focus the mind (as with time spent in the condemned cell - of which, luckily, I have no experience) wonderfully for serious thought on the matters in hand.....

The exercises in the book which were composed by me were initially created for my own benefit. The other exercises are ones I have practised over time and found to be the most effective. I sincerely hope other guitarists will gain some benefit from the following pages of thoughts, suggestions, studies and exercises.

Robin Hill 1999

'The success sometimes may come immediately but we must be ready to wait patiently even for what may look like an infinite length of time. The student who sets out with such a spirit of perseverance will surely find success and realization at last.'

Vivekananda (32)

Robin Hill was born in Huddersfield, Yorkshire, England and educated at Bolton School. He studied guitar at the Huddersfield College of Music and has participated in masterclasses with the eminent Venezuelan guitarist, **Alirio Diaz**. At Huddersfield Robin met fellow guitarist, **Peter Wiltschinsky**, and together they formed, in 1973, the **Hill/Wiltschinsky Guitar Duo**, a highly-successful partnership with a vast archive of recordings (they have recorded for **Teldec Classics, Hyperion, ASV, RCA, Telstar, Box Tree, IMP Classics, Carlton Classics, Erato** and many more). The duo have also made many broadcasts and have many international tours to their credit.

The duo's recent activities include performing **Joaquín Rodrigo's**, *'Concierto Madrigal'* with the **Royal Liverpool Philharmonic Orchestra,** recording their 40th. CD, *'The Sonatas of Antonio Soler'*, performing **Mario Castelnuovo-Tedesco's** *'Concerto for Two Guitars'* with the **B.B.C. Concert Orchestra (conductor - Barry Wordsworth)**, the **Irish National Symphony Orchestra (conductor - Albert Rosen)** and the **Caracas Symphony Orchestra** and many TV and radio appearances.

In 1997, Robin, who also composes, gave the UK première of his own, *'Concerto Primavera'* for guitar and marimba with the **Promontoire Chamber Orchestra (conductor - Ian Tracey)**.

Robin also gave the U.K. première of **Claude Bolling's**, *'Concerto for Classical Guitar and Jazz Piano Trio'* - a work he has recorded with his quartet, **Eklectica**.

In July 1998 he performed **Joaquín Rodrigo's**, *'Concierto de Aranjuez'* with the **Royal Liverpool Philharmonic Orchestra (conductor - Carl Davis)**, to an audience of 3,500.

In addition to these activities, Robin was also a member of the **B.B.C. Northern Radio Orchestra,** playing both electric and classical guitars, and has collaborated with artists as diverse as soprano **Lesley Garrett**, flautist **Atarah Ben Tovim**, the young British tenor and rising superstar, **Russel Watson**, rock bands **Jethro Tull** and **Deep Purple** and jazz/soul singer, **Madeline Bell**.

'As always, it was sheer pleasure to observe Robin Hill's remarkable fluent technique: everything looks easy when he plays it.' **Colin Cooper 'Classical Guitar'**

'There's nothing they (Hill/Wiltschinsky Duo) can't play. The whole evening constituted a breath of stimulating fresh air in a scene where so many duos lack the technical equipment to make it to the big time. for Robin Hill and Peter Wiltschinsky anything is possible.' **Colin Cooper 'Classical Guitar'**

'Wonderful for their (Hill/Wiltschinsky Duo) precision, touch and clarity of sound....refined virtuosity, the achievment of a long interpretive process.' **Il Giornale D'Italia (Rome)**

Contents.........

Chapter I - The Arpeggio..Page 5

Chapter II - The Scale..Page 31

Chapter III - The Slur...Page 52

Chapter IV - Performance and Practice......................Page 67

Appendix - Further study material.............................Page 75

(Esercizio No. 3, 100 right hand exercises,)

Acknowledgements

I would like to thank my wife, Anna, for her constant support and encouragement in all my musical activities.

I would also like to express my thanks to Graham and Elizabeth Wade for their enthusiastic help in the preparation of this book.

I would like to thank my parents, Marie and Derrick Hill, for making the many, many hours I have spent in the guitar gymnasium possible.

I would also like to thank Peter Wiltschinsky, my duo partner for 25 years, we have learnt a great deal from each other.

Robin Hill 1999

CHAPTER 1.
The Arpeggio

Let's firstly examine the methods I have used and found effective in the practice of the following musical examples:

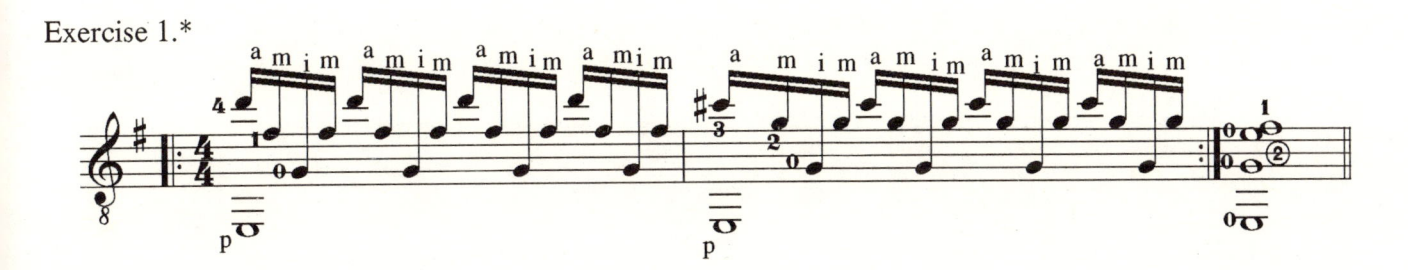

Exercise 1.*

One of the most basic and important principles in guitar technique is economy of movement. This, naturally, applies not only to both hands but to any other part of the body involved in the production of the note. We have, therefore, to create an effective playing mechanism. If one considers the right hand in playing Exercise 1, the hand itself should be completely stable with the knuckles immobile. I regard the index finger knuckle as the focal point imagining it as the fulcrum of the right hand, keeping the other knuckles parallel to the strings. The fingers themselves move in a minimal way each one maintaining a consistent trajectory and starting the beginning of the exercise in contact with the string it is to play. The movement is one of pressing, rather than hitting against, the string. I would initially practise this exercise silently just touching the strings but without producing any sound. This helps to establish playing 'from the string' and also using the minimum amount of movement. This silent practice should also be accompanied by 'hearing' the notes mentally and thus reinforcing the inner ear. Indeed it is always good practice to 'hear' the notes in one's head a split second before playing them:

'It's a question of knowing what sort of sound you're going to produce before you make it. It's because you've put your finger there, that that is the sound that will come out.'
John Williams (1)

'One of the most important ideas in guitar technique is the association between the ear and the hands. In the end it is the sound one desires that should motivate and guide every move the hands make.'
Pepe Romero (2)

Exercise 2.

Exercise 3.

* from '100 Right Hand Exercises' - a complete version of which appears in Appendix.

The first exercise can be practised in the following ways: 1. Without bass line (resting thumb on bass E or A string). 2. Tirando (free stroke on treble notes) apoyando (rest stroke on bass). This is a very important technique to master. The thumb in playing a rest stroke not only makes the bass line more resonant, but also, due to following through and resting on A string, gives extra right hand stability. 3. Accenting 'a' finger with rest stroke with rest stroke in bass. 4. All free strokes. 5. Varying dynamics.

Exercises 2 and 3 feature the same arpeggio with different bass lines. This is to facilitate independence between thumb and fingers and introduces the important technique of damping bass notes by plucking and immediately going back to rest on same bass string. Again, try practising treble and bass separately at first then combine. When damping bass, it is not possible to play a rest stroke with the thumb. The bass notes should be played quite forcefully in 2 and 3.

Exercise 4 (more variations)

Exercise 5.

Exercise 6.

Exercise 7.

Exercise 8.

Exercise 9.

Exercise 10.

These exercises should be taken at a slow ($\quarternote = 60$) tempo initially gradually increasing the tempo. Practise with a metronome is recommended (but not all the time). The exercises should be played with fluency and technical command, accuracy is paramount.

Exercises 11 - 20 deal with changes in rhythmic groupings of arpeggios and feature quintuplets, sextuplets, septuplets as well as the more usually encountered semiquavers. Aim for equality of timbre and do not allow the thumb's movement to displace overall right hand position.

Exercise 11.

Exercise 12.

Exercise 13.

Exercise 14.

Exercise 15.

Exercise 16.

Exercise 17.

Exercise 18.

Exercise 19.

Exercise 20.

During the practice of these exercises remind yourself of the goals you are trying to achieve: 1. Right hand stability without rigidity. 2. Minimum movement. 3. Varied right hand techniques. i.e. rest strokes and free strokes. 4. Dynamic variations. The creation of an efficient and reliable playing mechanism.

Variety in practice is important, always try to surprise your fingers with new challenges and studies. Amongst the finest and most effective exercises for the arpeggio must be the ones devised by the great Francisco Tárrega. Make these studies part of your regular practice and you will reap enormous benefits. As with the preceding exercises the same goals apply. The left hand keeps to the same pattern throughout, and must be consistent in it's plane of movement, exerting the minimum amount of pressure to produce a clear note. Play the bass notes with rest strokes, free strokes and staccato (damping attack).

Francisco Tárrega

Exercise 21.

Exercise 22.

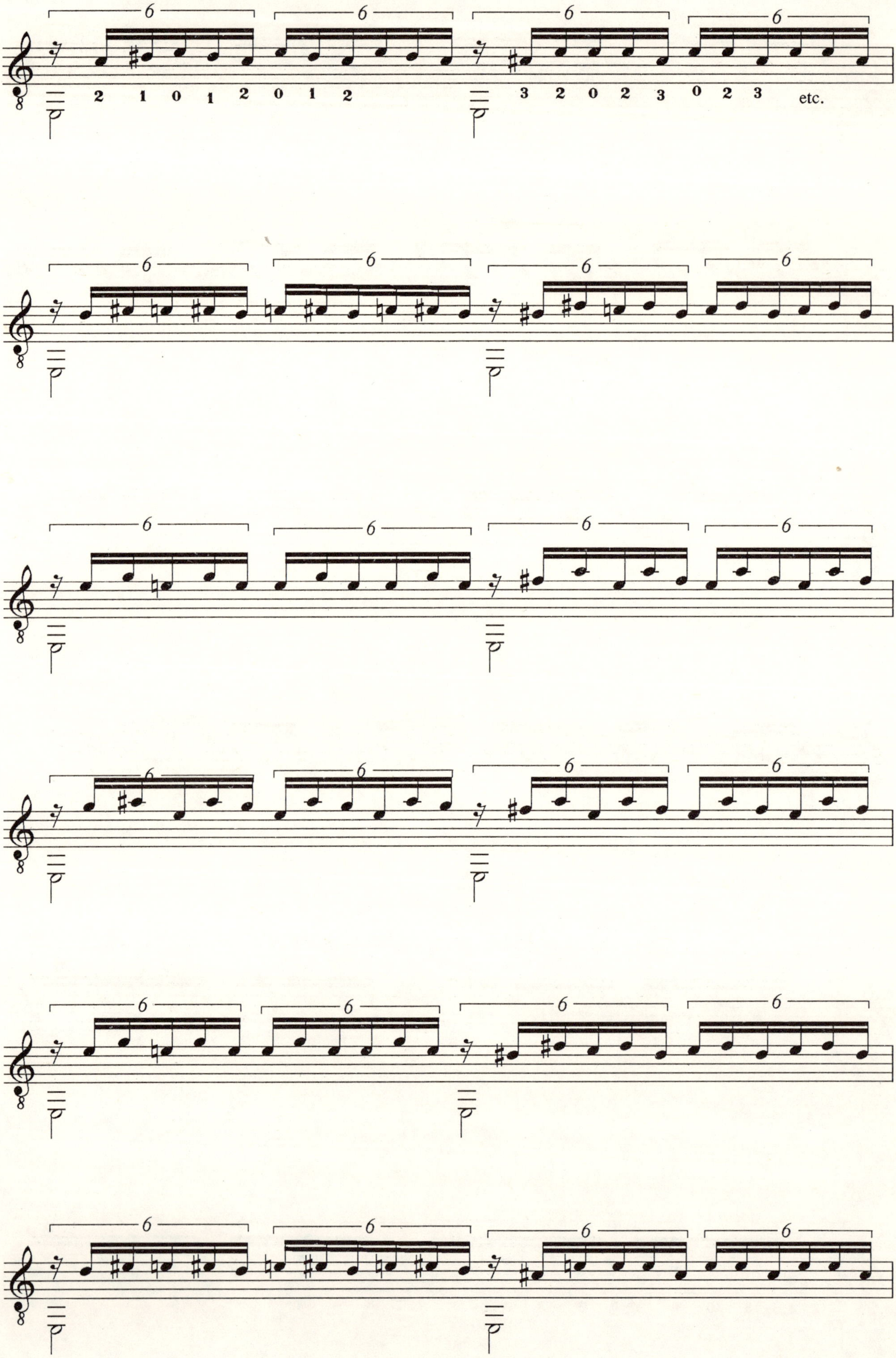
2 1 0 1 2 0 1 2
3 2 0 2 3 0 2 3
etc.

Exercise 23.

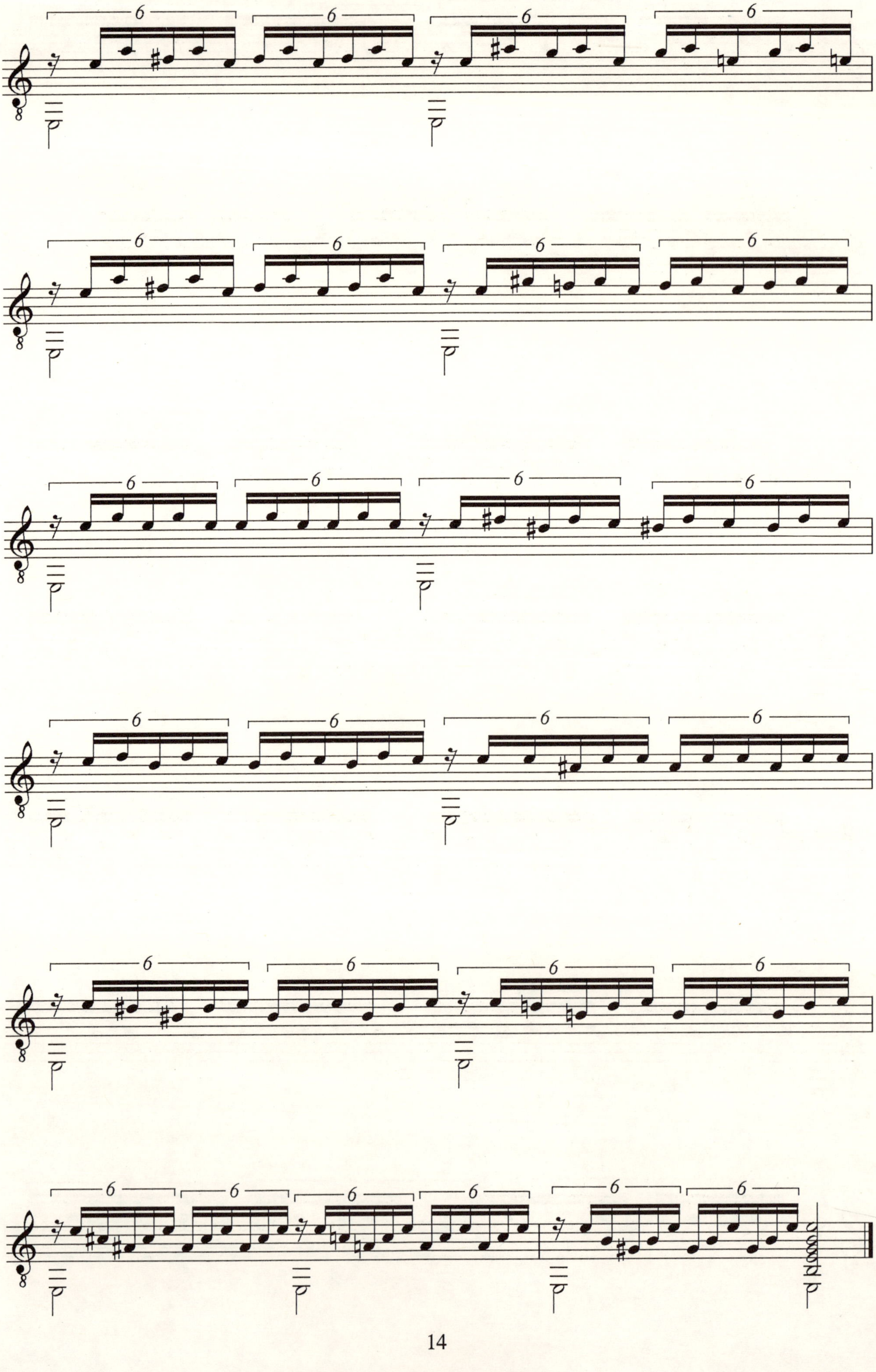
6
6
6
6

Exercise 24.

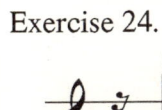

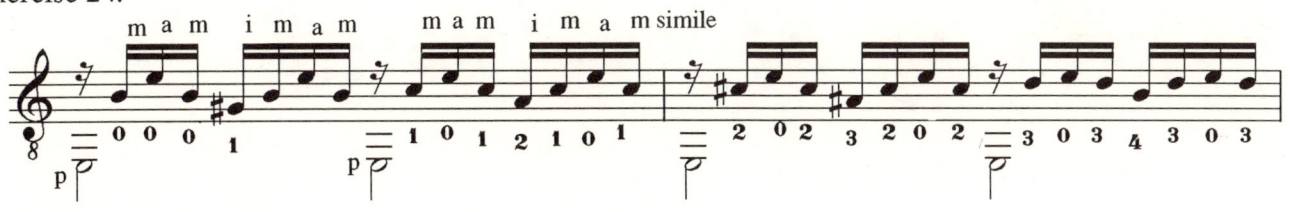

Exercise 25.

Exercise 26.

Exercise 27.

Exercise 28.

Exercise 29.

Exercise 30.

The following is an extract from the 3rd movement of my 'Concerto Primavera'. I have found it to be a useful arpeggio study. As always, practise slowly - the eventual tempo is fast but possible!

6th = D

*Hold this down from beginning.

18

19

Always practise attentively, I have never agreed with musicians who advocate practising whilst watching TV! Also beware of the deadly routine of wading, without concentration, through studies and exercises.

'I have to be present at every note I play'

Andrés Segovia (3)

'Regard routine for nothing and reason for everything'

Fernando Sor (4)

Meanwhile, back to Tárrega with some extra fingerings of mine - these are excellent for developing r.h. stamina and dexterity...practise No. 31.: mi, im, am, ma, imam, mima, mami, amim, pima, pimi, free stroke in treble, rest stroke in bass, and all free strokes. Use backs of a and e (little finger) also.

Exercise 31.

Francisco Tárrega
etc. as in preceding examples up and down the neck.

Exercise 32.

Exercise 33.

Right hand fingering for No. 34. consists of the following combinations: im, mi, ma, am, imam, mima, mami, amim, pimi, pima and also backs of ae (alternately) as in rasgueado.

Exercise 34.

Exercise 35.

In addition to indicated fingering practise No.36 : mima, mami, amim, im, mi, ma and am.

Exercise 36.

Plus mamama, amamam.

Exercise 37.

21

Plus pama, pmam
Exercise 38.

etc. as in preceding examples up and down the neck.

Also use fingering : pmi, pma, pam, pmi pma, pma pmi, pam pim.

Exercise 39.

etc. as in preceding examples up and down the neck.

Exercise 40.

etc. as in preceding examples up and down the neck.

Next, we will consider arpeggios which require more complex fingering patterns. e.g.:

Robin Hill

Exercise 41.

Exercise 42.

Exercise 43.

Exercise 44.

There follows a study composed with the express purpose of practising these more complex arpeggio configurations:

Study No.1

Robin Hill

♩. = 80

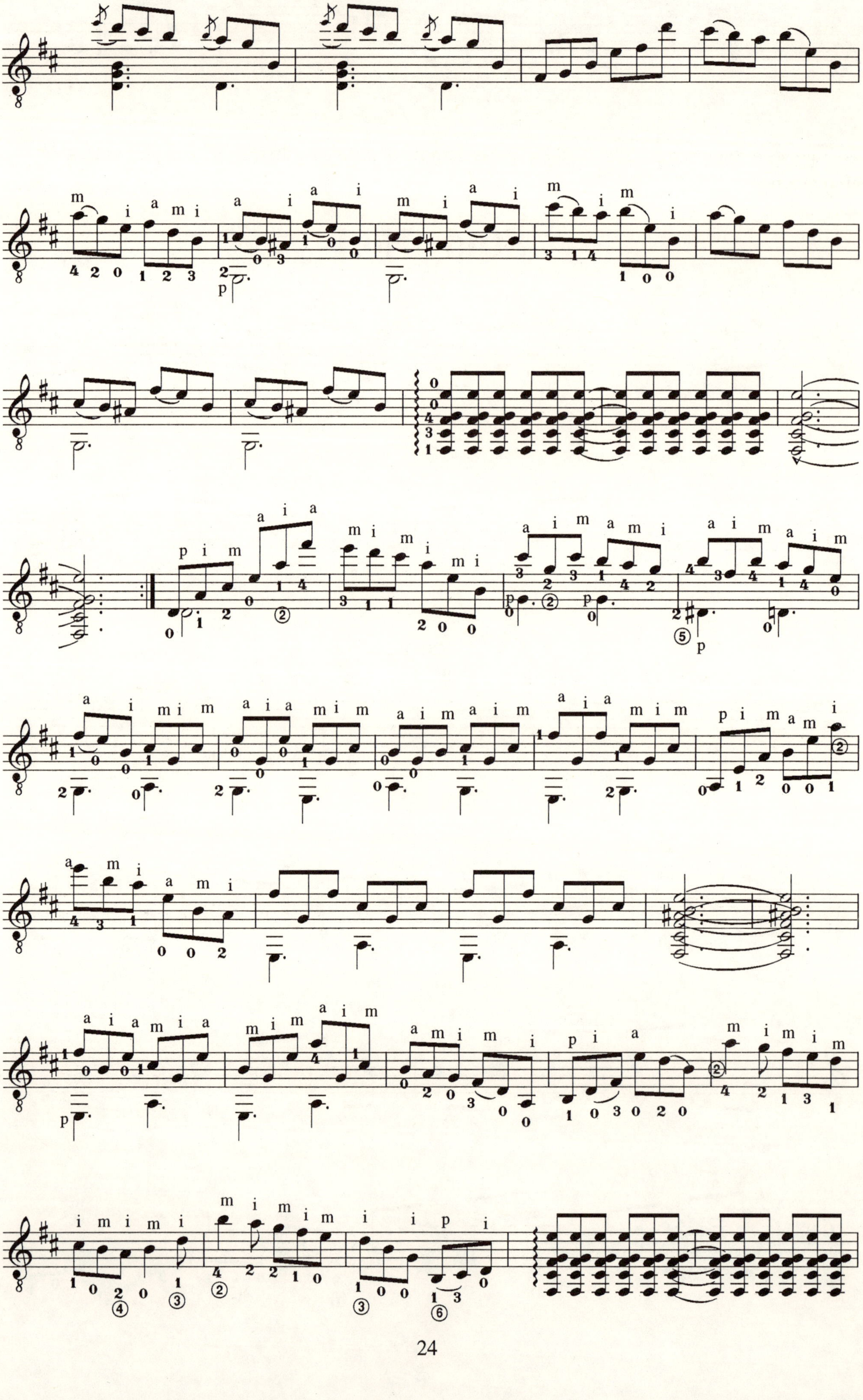

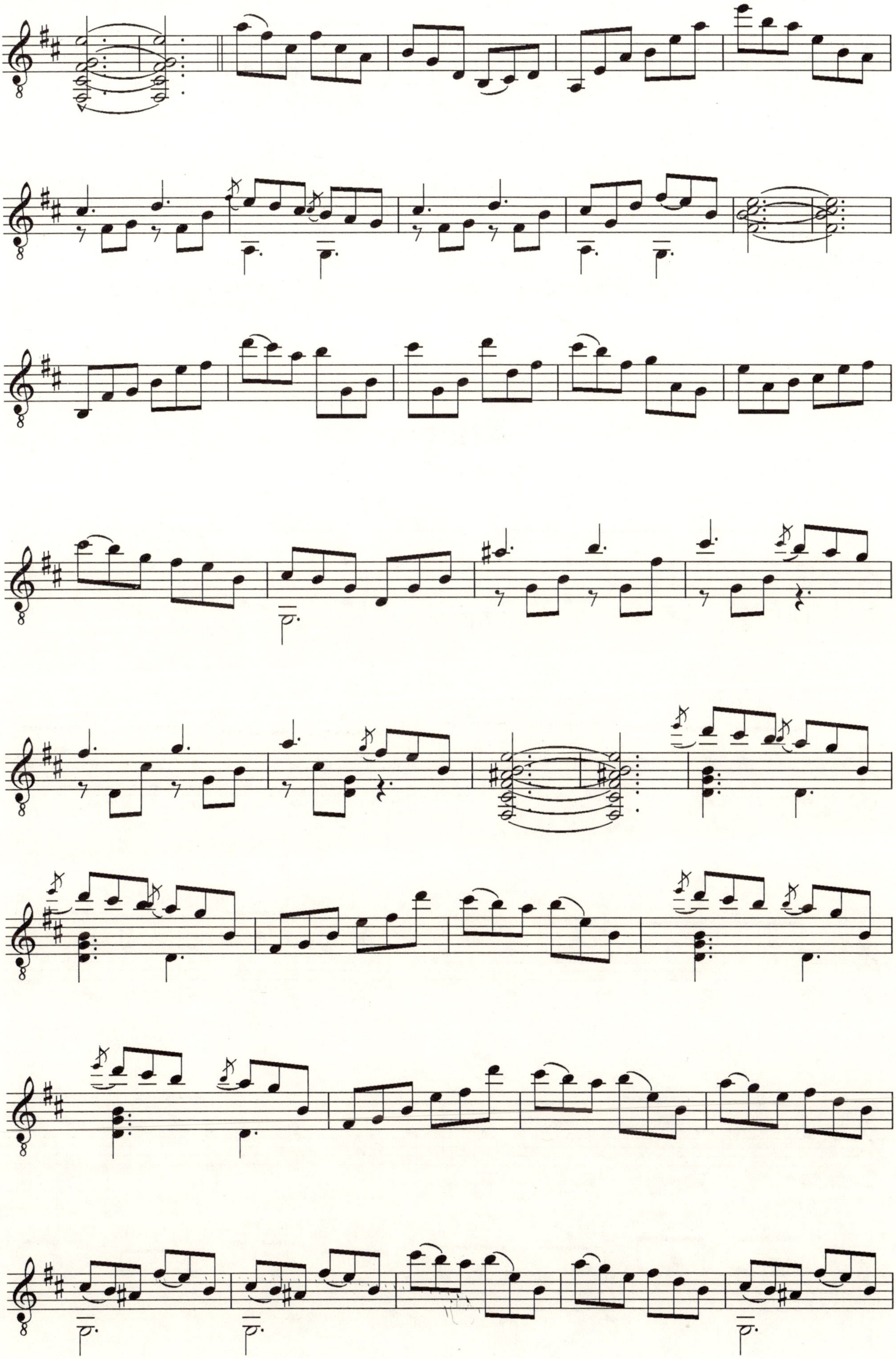

I have found the following arrangement to be particularly helpful in strengthening and improving right hand flexibility and fluency. It is the third movement from Antonio Vivaldi's 'Concerto in D'. Here I have added bass notes throughout, thus demanding the same fluency from the three right hand fingers (ami) as previously demanded from thumb, index and middle fingers. (pim)
This provides an enjoyable workout for the right hand...

Allegro
Antonio Vivaldi
(arranged by Robin Hill)

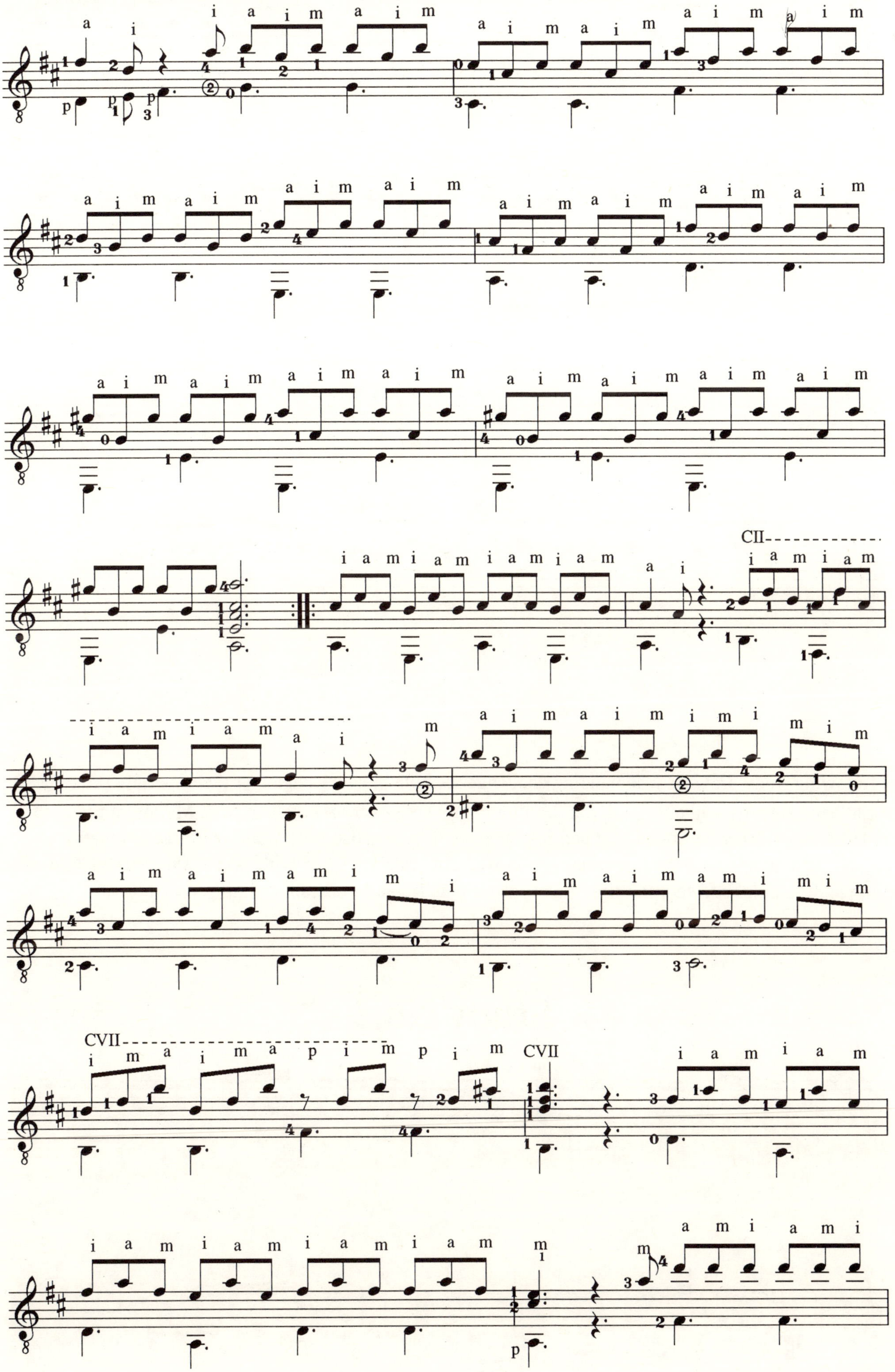
CII
CVII
CVII

The following study provides a demanding challenge for both hands. Remember the important principles:
1. Right hand stability without rigidity. 2. Minimum movements from both hands. 3. Minimum pressure from left hand. 4. Hear the sound first before you make it. 5. Practise slowly and resist the temptation to attempt final tempo until the fingerings and movements can be played with ease at slow tempo. 6.Ideally, memorize the studies and scrutinize your performance. 6. Record yourself. 7. Enjoy yourself!

Study No.2
Robin Hill

29

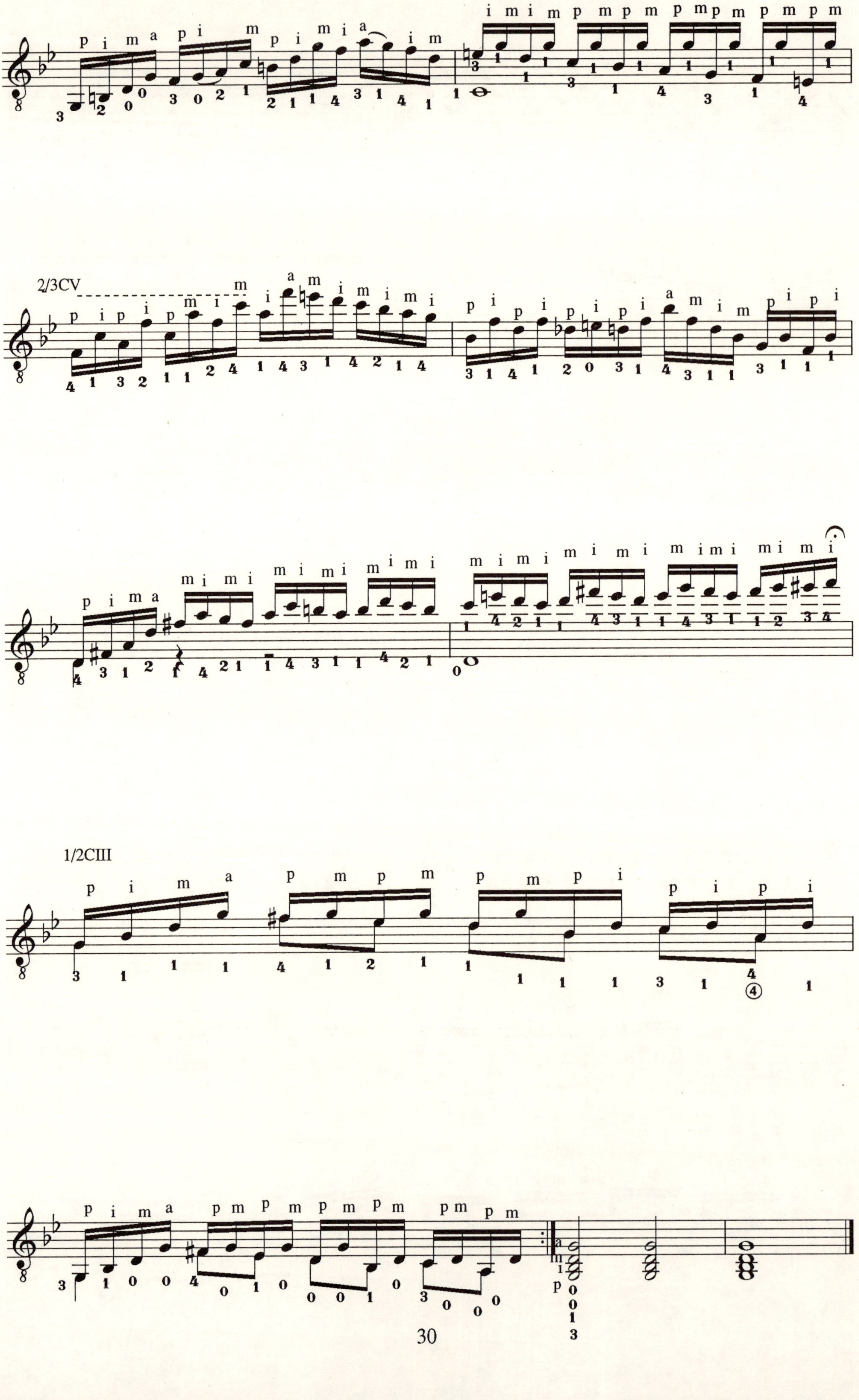
2/3CV
1/2CIII

Chapter II.
The Scale.

'The practice of scales enables one to solve a greater number of technical problems in a shorter time than the study of any other exercise.'

Andrés Segovia (5)

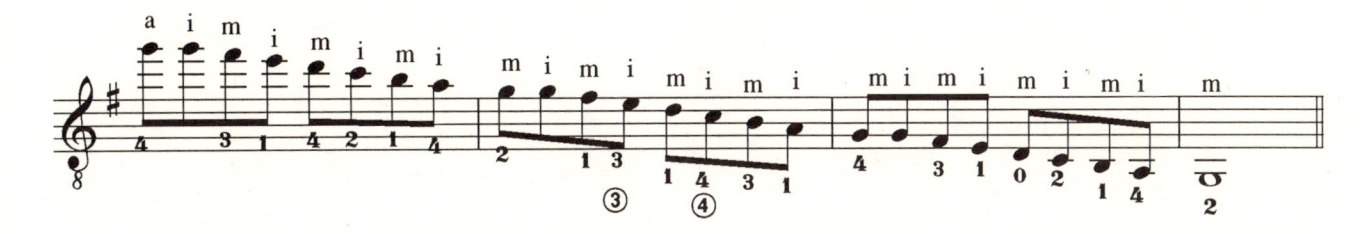

Exercise No.1.

There are many different methods of playing scales on the guitar. As a general rule, if alternating between i and m, it is undesirable to cross strings using mi when ascending and im when descending. It is not always possible to avoid this situation, but this principle should be seriously considered. The guitarist must learn a more flexible approach to scale playing than moving the same patterns (using entirely stopped fingering) up and down the neck. The above example demonstrates one way of avoiding this particular problem (using the 'a' finger once). In other words, we must practise difficult crossings, but avoid them when possible. The following example uses thumb, open strings and stretched out left hand fingering to avoid undesirable crossings. It can be played using both rest stroke and free stroke. When the thumb is used it should immediately go back to rest on the string it has just played in order to dampen it.

Exercise No.2.

Allegro

This example, by Francisco Tárrega, is a very useful exercise. The fingering is mine, to avoid difficult crossings, Tárrega advocates practising this im, mi, ma and am. this should, of course be practised also.

Exercise No.3.

There are, invariably, various solutions to the same problem. Remember that the printed fingering is never sacred! There are usually viable alternatives. During scale playing the same principles of economy of movement and right and left hand stability, as discussed in the previous chapter, apply.

> *'In all playing, the notions of plucking the strings should be all in the fingers and not in the palm or arm. The right hand should not bounce with the movements of the fingers, nor should it be moved away from the strings during the fingers' strokes by lifting the forearm or bending the wrist.'* Pepe Romero (6)

With these thoughts in mind, let's practise the following study, taking care the thumb strokes don't displace the right hand position.

Study No. 4

Robin Hill

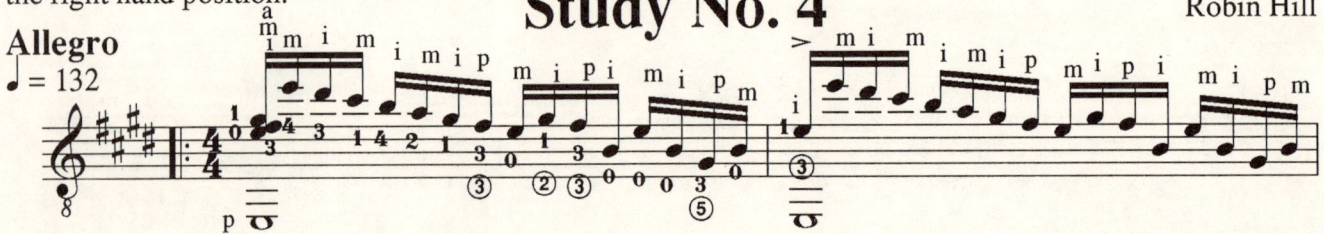

Allegro
♩ = 132

33

In some contexts, notably Elizabethan and Baroque music, it can be stylistically and technically appropriate to use alternate p.i or p.m (free stroke) the effect is incisive, take this example of Scarlatti:

Sonata K.141

Domenico Scarlatti

(Trans. for 2 guitars - Robin Hill)

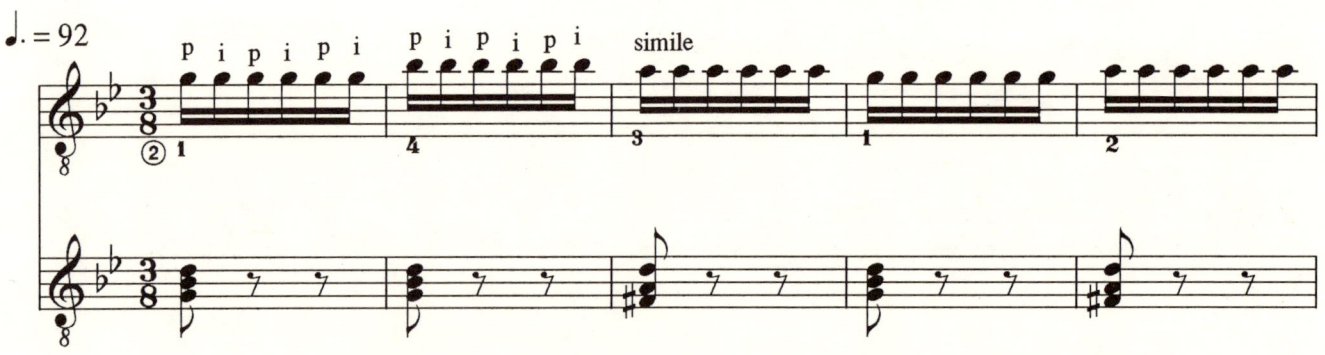

Allegro

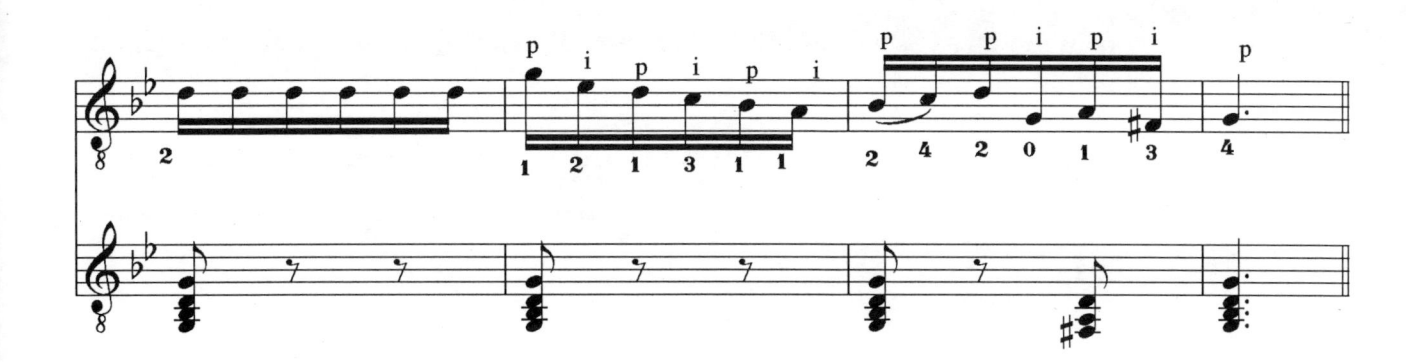

The same fingering can be applied to this galliard for two lutes by John Johnson:

La Vecchia Galliard

Allegro

(Trans. Robin Hill)

John Johnson

Capos at 3rd. fret.

A effective triplet variation of this fingering is shown here in the context of a Jota variation:

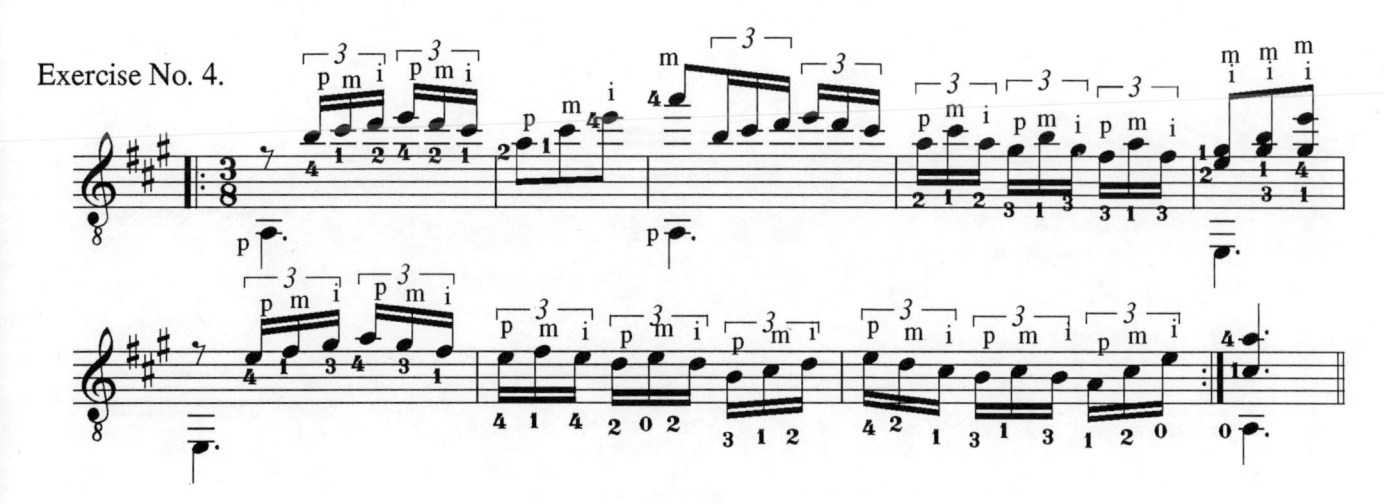

Exercise No. 4.

The following is a good warm-up and stamina building exercise. It should be practised both free and rest stroke:

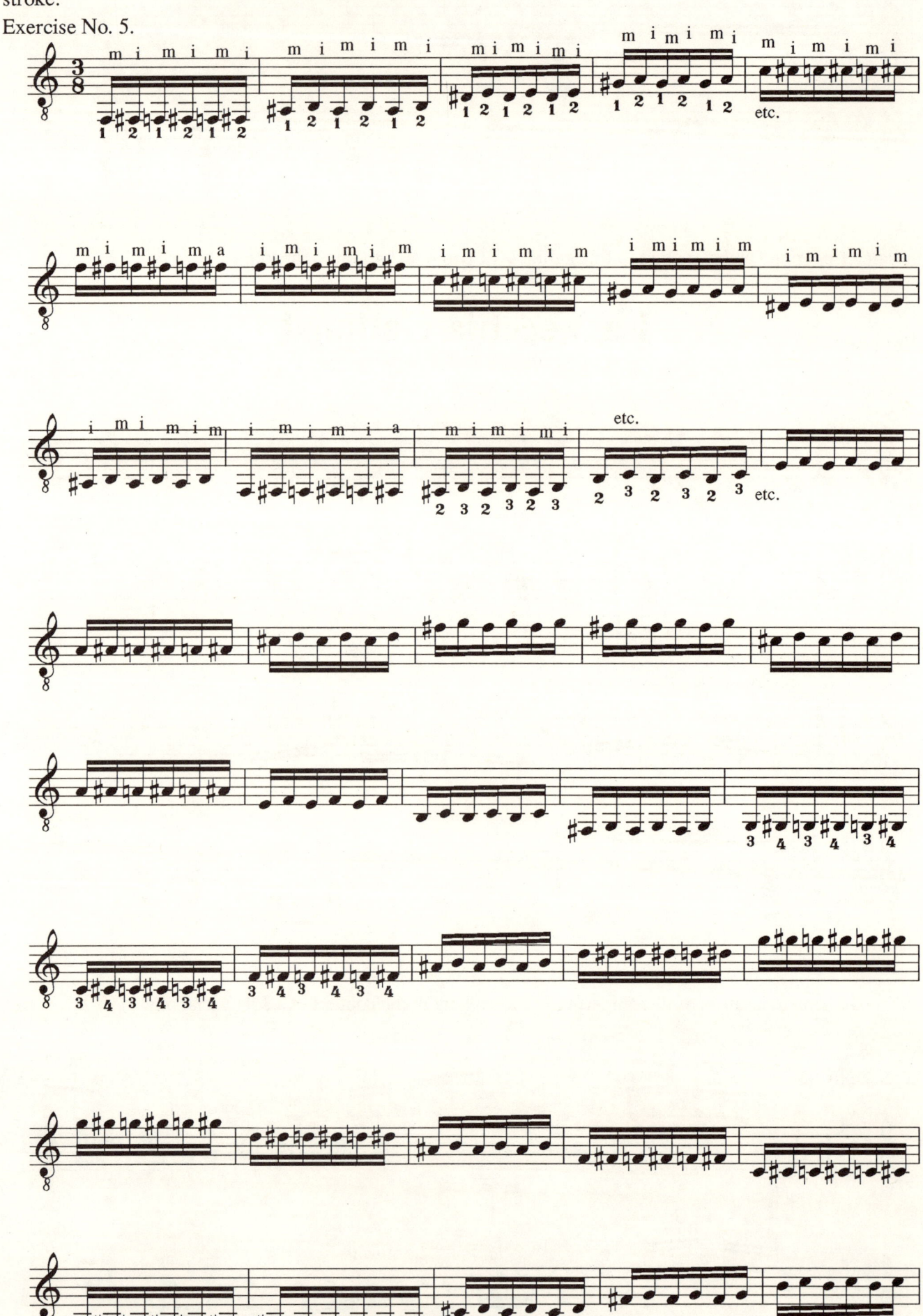

Exercise No. 5.

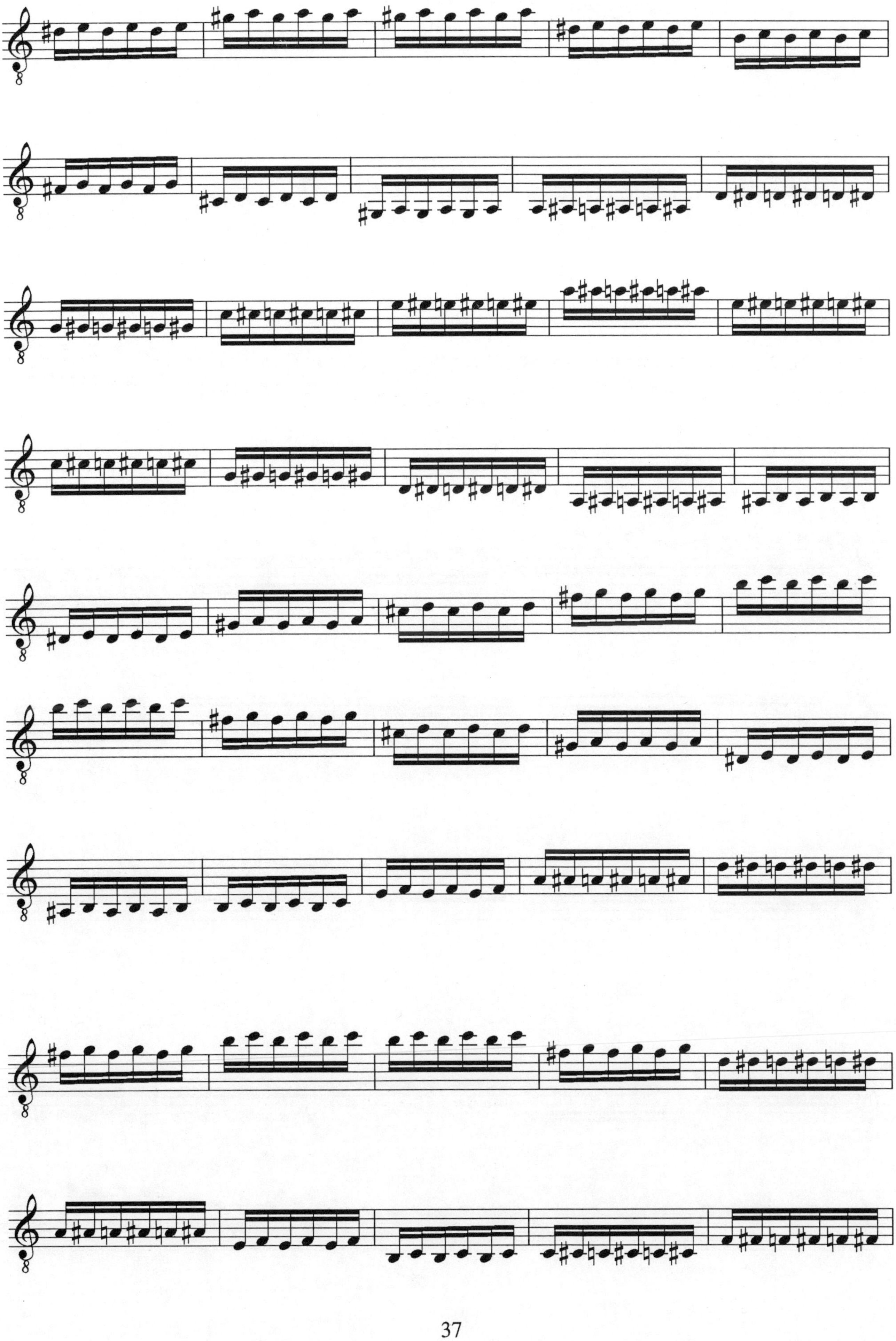

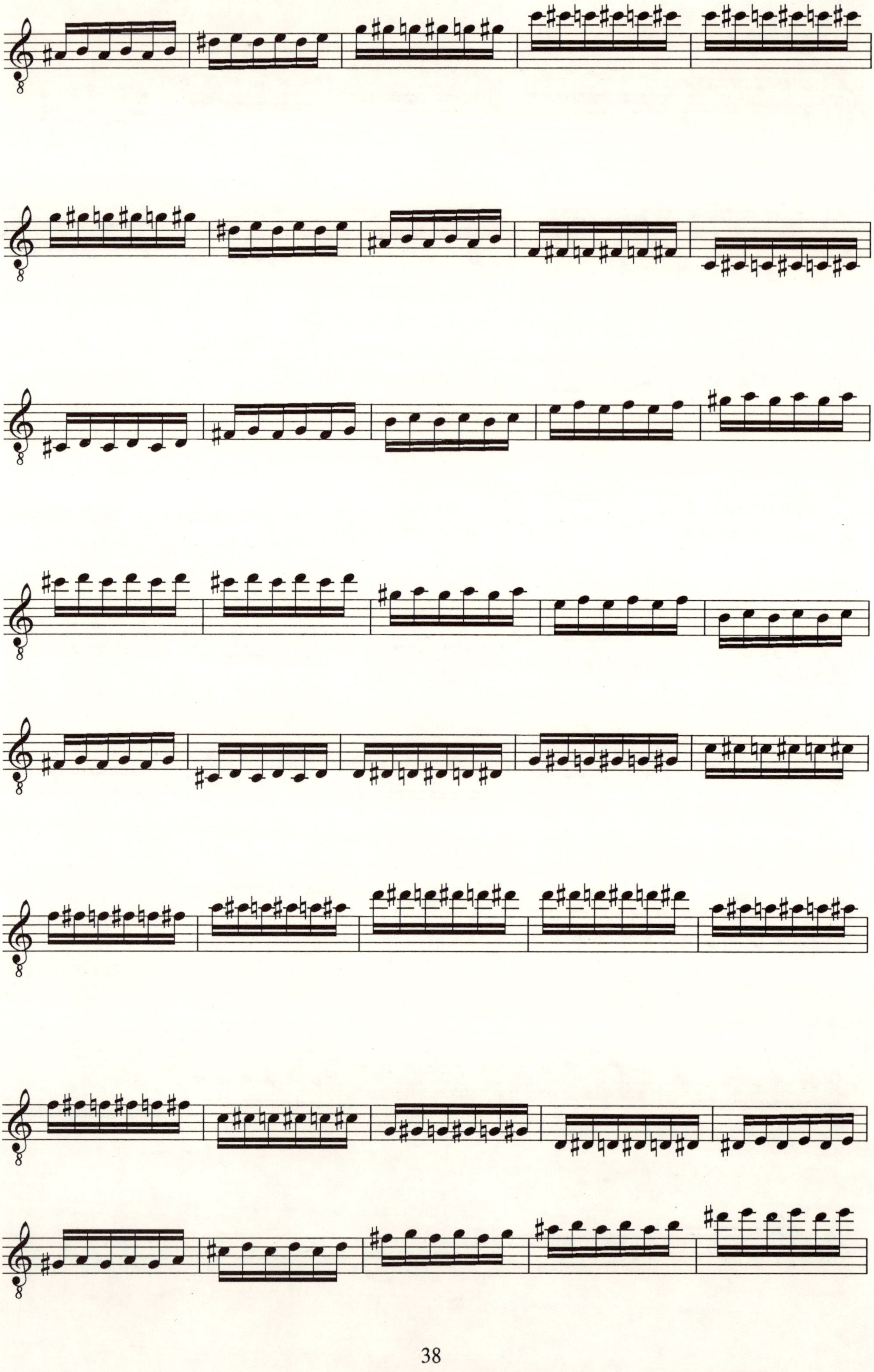

I have also found that practice with the backs of the nails i.e. movement in the opposite direction to the normal stroke, is extremely beneficial. It has a similar effect to practising rasgueados and generally leads to improving the right hand's 'feel good' factor. Try it! Movements should be rapid and forceful, as in rasgueado.

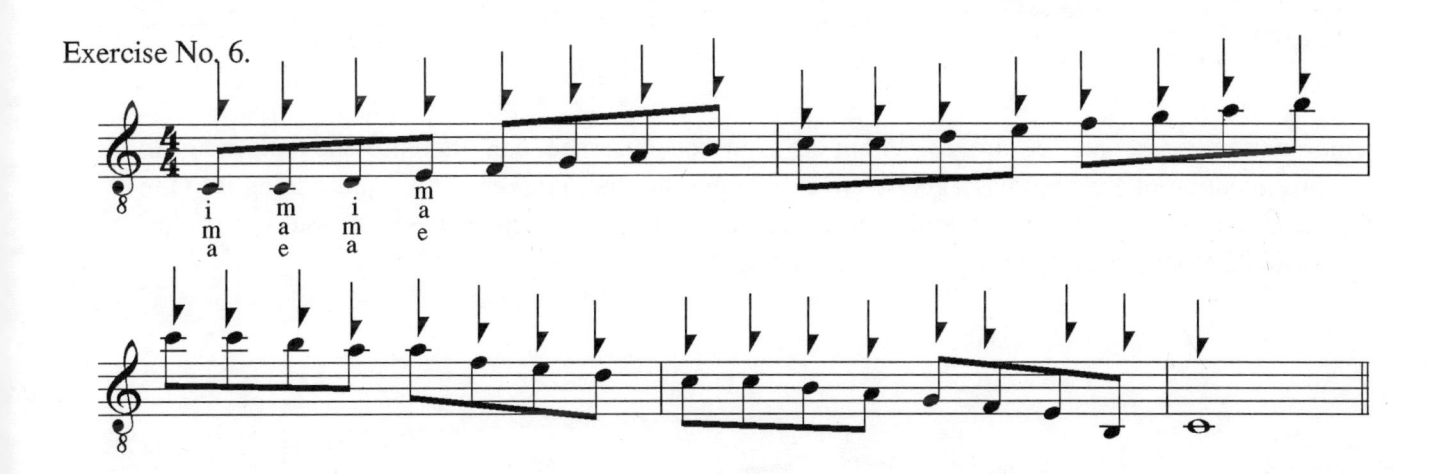

Exercise No. 6.

This exercise concentrates on string crossing. Practise this using light rest strokes:

Exercise No. 7.

This scale exercise flows as I have avoided awkward string crossings, to enable the player to concentrate on the salient points of scale technique. Remember! Minimum movement in both hands - it can be played rest or free stroke, or a combination of the two. There should be very little, if any, difference in right hand position for the two techniques..

Exercise No. 8.

A combination of rest and free strokes, within the same scale passage, can often provide a pleasing solution as to the execution of a certain passage. Often, by playing the first note rest stroke and joining it to the second with a slur and then playing the remaining notes free stroke (with sometimes the final note rest stroke) the the phrasing and tonal weight of the passage is just right:

Exercise No.9.

Exercise No.10. (Practise up and down each string)

Exercise No.11.

As with the arpeggios in Chapter 1, all these scale exercises can be practised silently! This pressing against, but not sounding the string encourages and reinforces the most efficient playing action and sharpens the ear.

'For these abstract exercises I mute the violin and put a piece of tissue under the strings. I could say that to practise with a heavy mute or, as I once did, with a soaped bow, saves my ear from being dulled with a surfeit of sound, and that this self-imposed continence makes the pleasure of performing aloud all the keener. Beyond that, however, mime obliges me to internalize the music until I can 'hear' it in my digits, muscles and joints, until the body becomes a sort of aural intelligence, an instrument perfectly tuned and playing independently of me, a pure voice.'

Yehudi Menuhin (7)

Exercise No.12.

Francisco Tárrega

repeat same fingering up and down the neck.

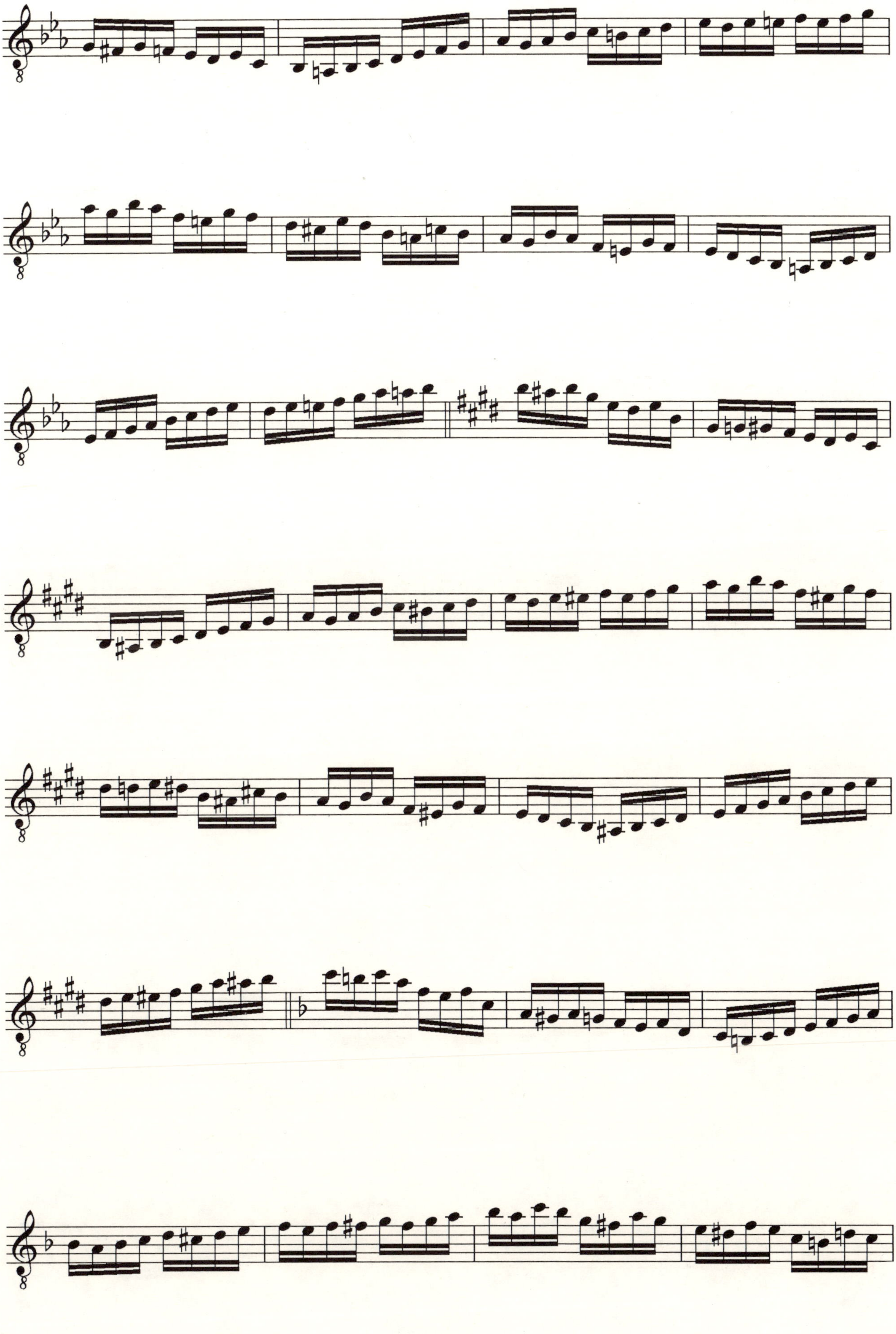

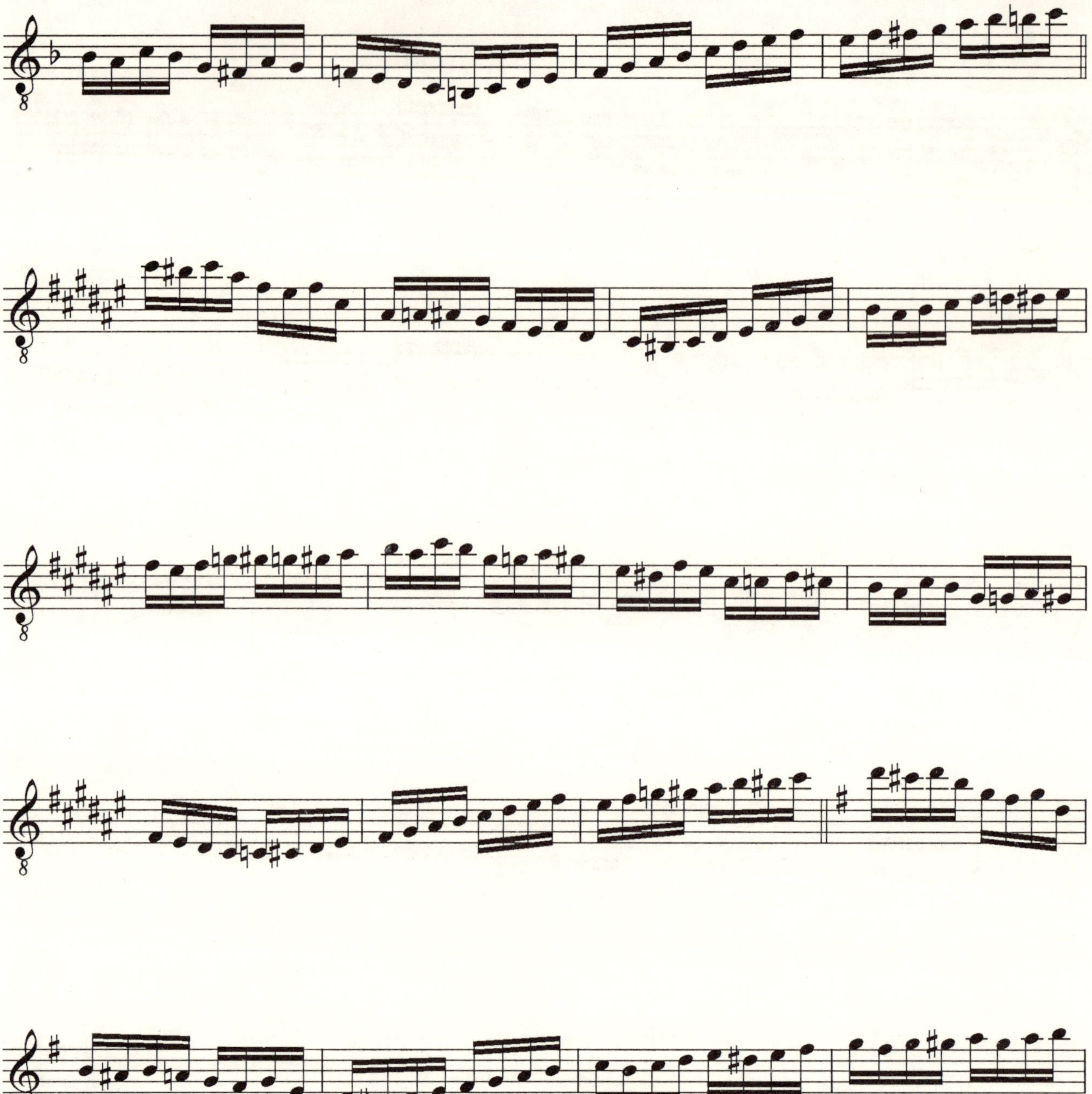

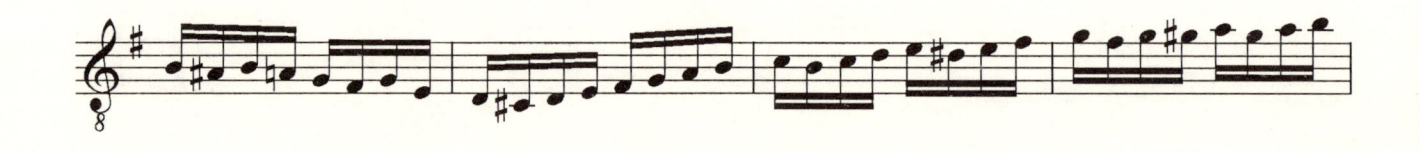

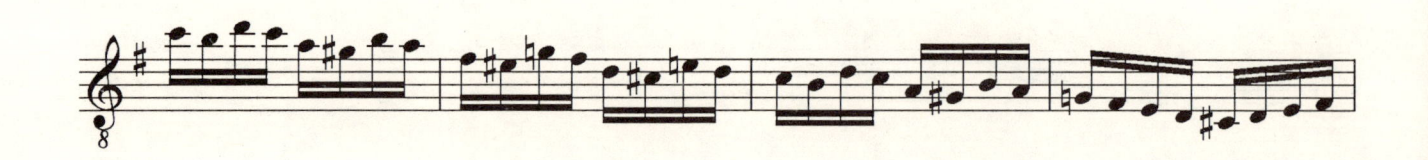

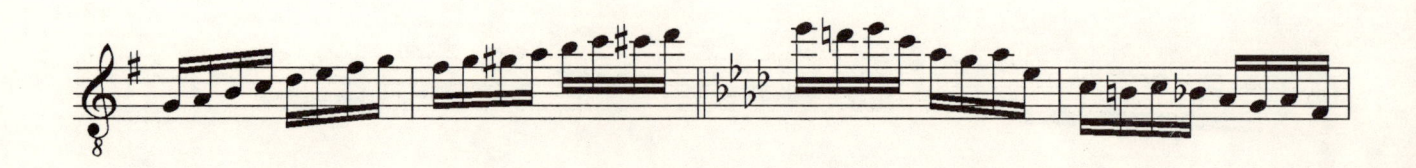

and down the neck chromatically through the same keys.

♩ = 152

Exercise No.13.

46

It is difficult to imagine a more demanding scale workout than Nicolo Paganini's 'Moto Perpetuo'.
I have transposed it from C major to A major and fingered it to facilitate fluency and velocity! Good luck!

Moto Perpetuo

(transcribed by Robin Hill)

Nicolo Paganini

Allegro vivace

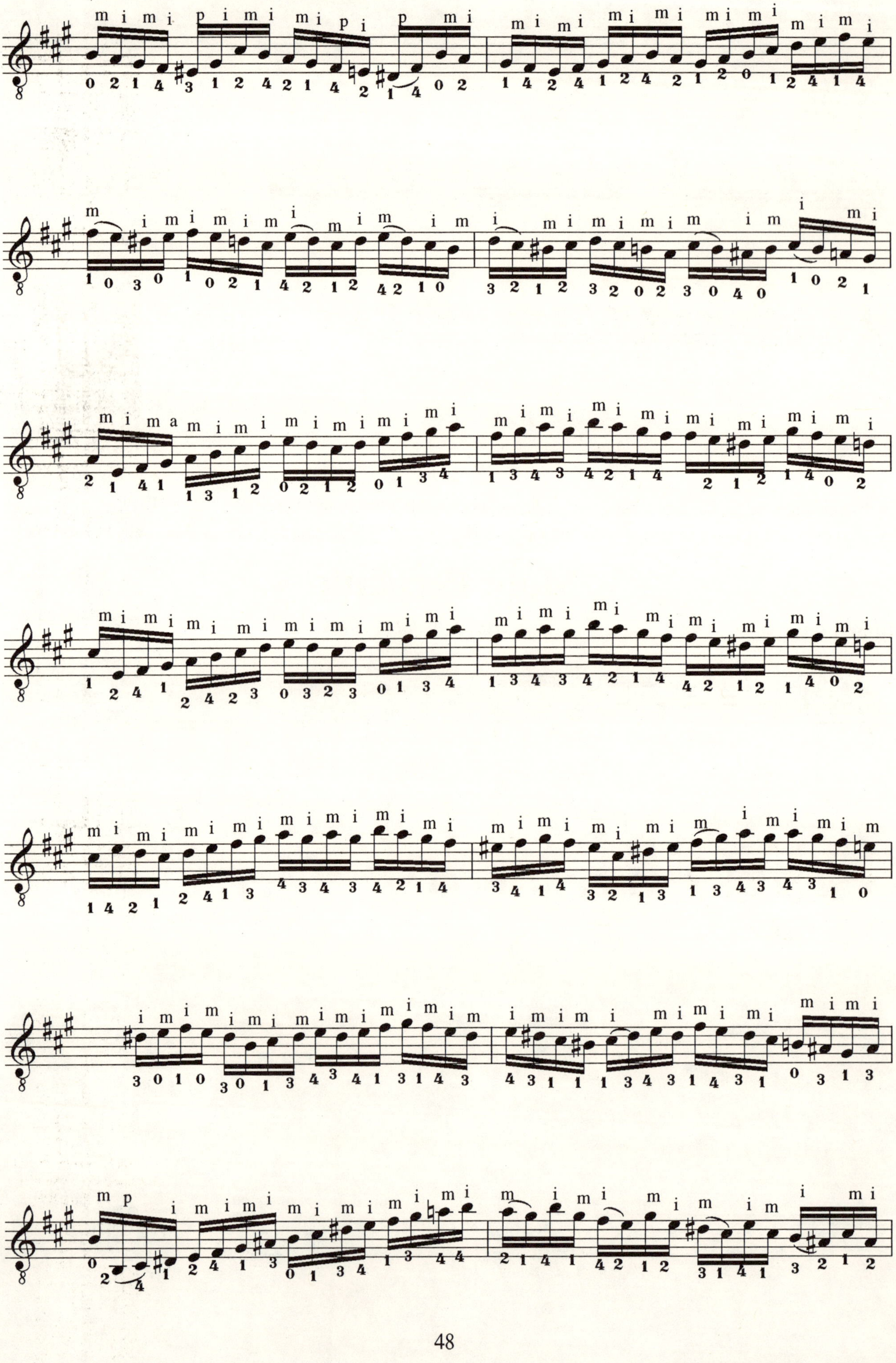

49

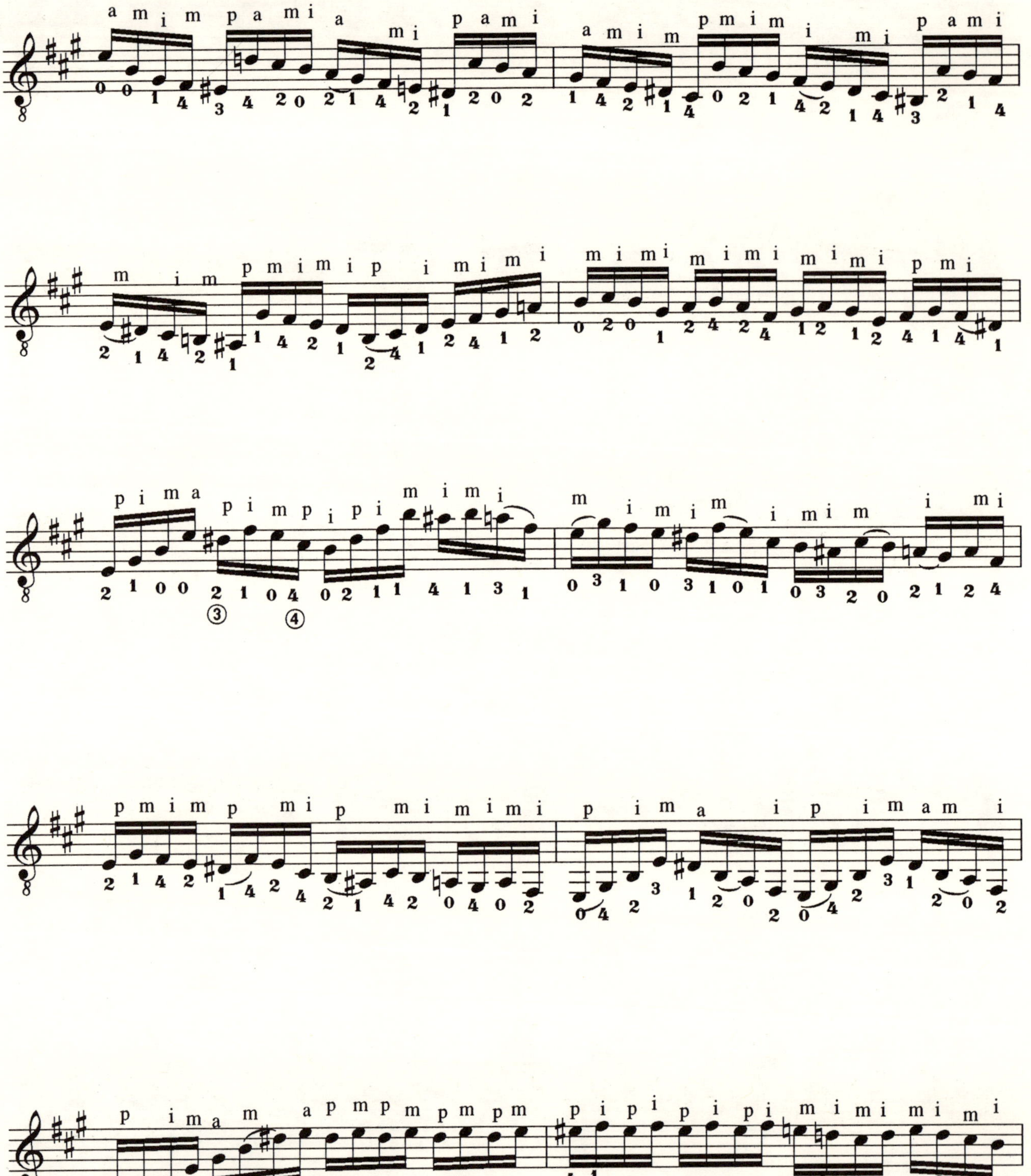

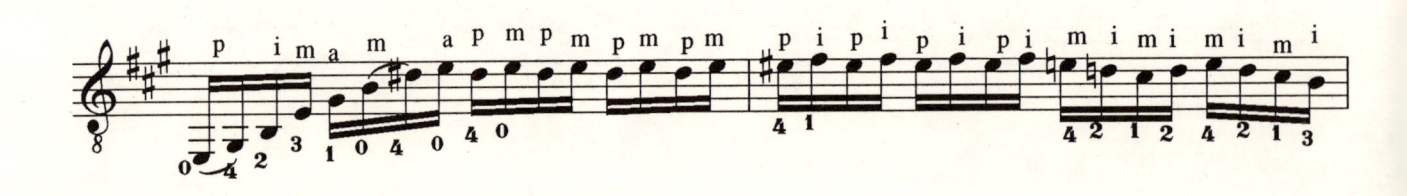

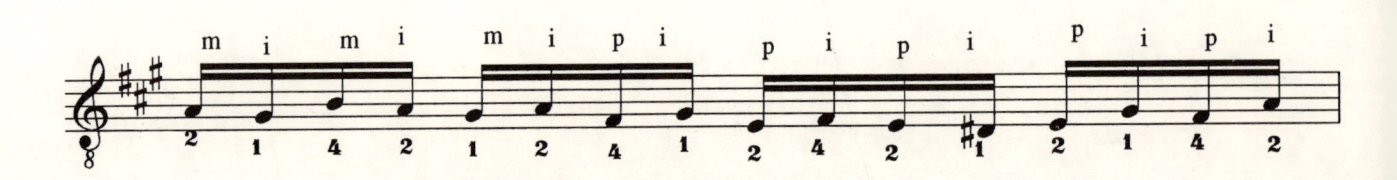

When practising major and minor diatonic scales try playing along with the metronome (on the offbeat is a good exercise) and also using various rhythms:

Chapter III.
All Manner of Slurs

Pull-offs and hammer-ons are an essential part of technique, and, as we have seen with arpeggios and scales, rely on economy of movement, flexibility and controlled strength for successful execution. The following exercises (1 - 3) are by Francisco Tárrega. The left hand knuckles should always be kept parallel to the strings with fingers poised above the notes they are about to produce. They should be played slowly and evenly with as much legato as possible.

Exercise No.1.(Pull-offs)

and back chromatically
down the neck.

Exercise No.2.

up and down the neck
chromatically

Exercise No.3.

Exercise No.4. (Hammer-ons)

Exercise No.5.

Exercise No.6.

Exercise No.7.

Exercise No.8.

etc. up and down the neck chromatically

Exercise No.9.

Continue up and down each string.

Exercise No.10.

etc. up and down the neck chromatically

Study No. 5

Robin Hill

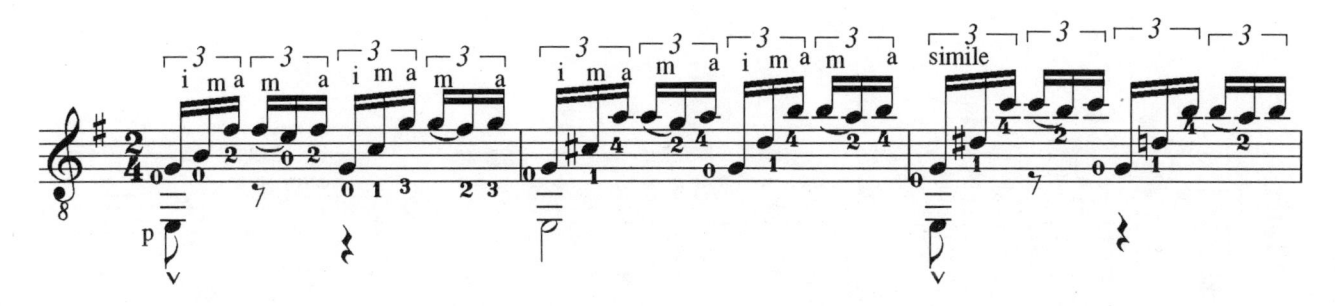

♩ = 84

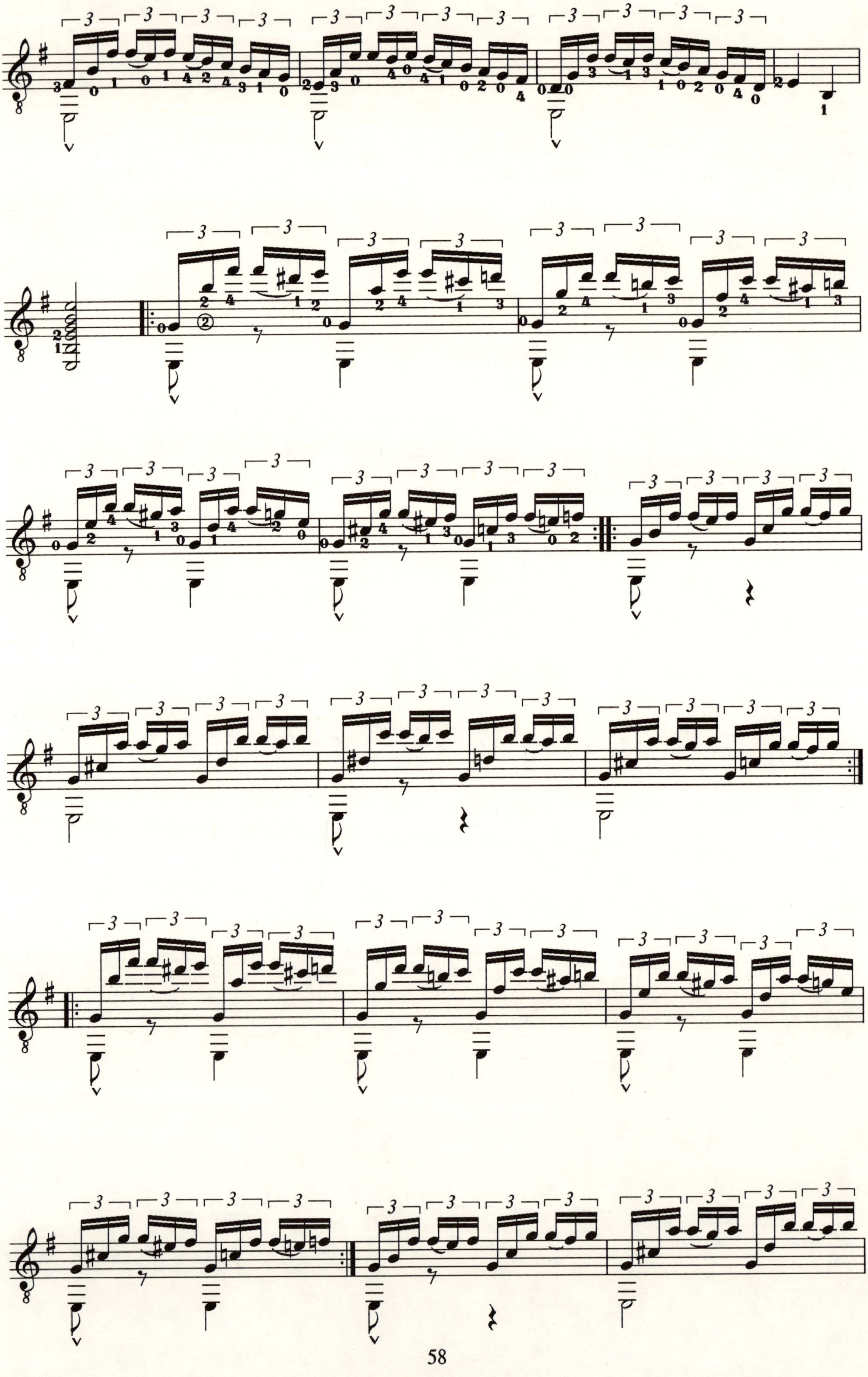
3

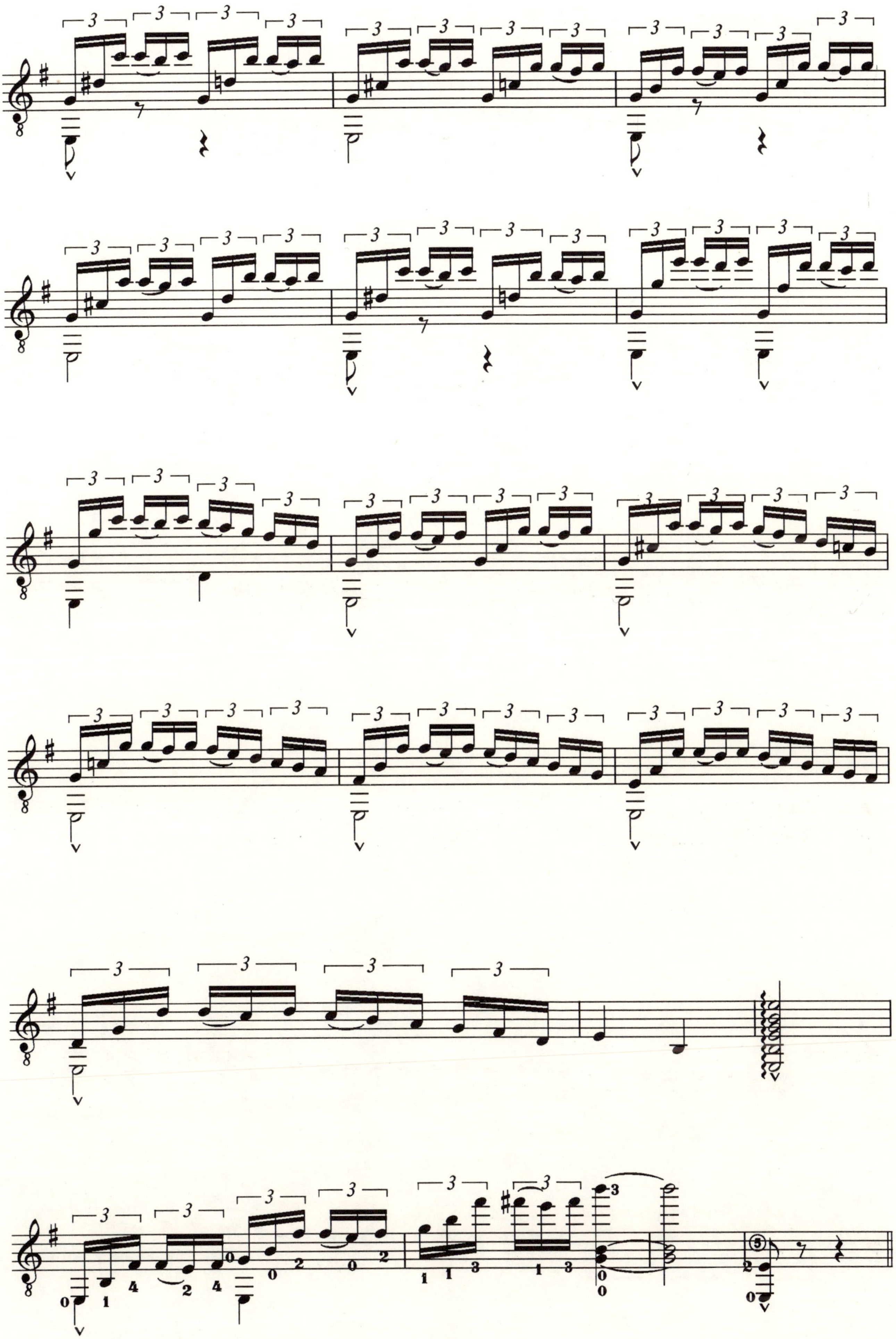

The following exercises by Tárrega are also very important for the development and maintenance of the slurring technique:

Exercise No. 11.

Exercise No. 12.

Exercise No. 13.

Exercise No. 14.

Exercise No. 15.

etc. up and down the neck chromatically

Exercise No. 16.

The following Tárrega exercise combines arpeggios, pull-offs and hammer-ons. Although the emphasis is mainly on the left hand, don't forget to observe all the fundamentals for good right hand technique mentioned in Chapter 1.

Exercise No. 17.

Exercise No. 18.

Exercise No. 19.

♩ = 250

Exercise No. 20.

66

Chapter IV.

Performance and Practice
A Collection of Thoughts

I firmly believe that attaining the balance between self-confidence and self-doubt is one of the artist's most important challenges:

'It constantly remains a source of disappointment to me that my drawings are not yet what I want them to be, the difficulties are indeed numerous and great, and cannot be overcome at once. To make progress is a kind of miner's work; it doesn't advance as quickly as one would like, and others also expect, but as one stands before such a task, the basic necessities are patience and faithfulness. In fact, I do not think much about the difficulties, because if one thought of them too much one would get stunned or disturbed.'

Vincent Van Gogh (8)
(letter to Theo)

If Vincent had not felt like this about his work it would have, indeed, been a surprise. This sense of striving and self-dissatisfaction provide the essential impetus to spur the artist to further and higher achievements. Eventually, as we all know, he did get the balance wrong, he did become stunned and disturbed, and the world lost one of it's greatest artists. We all have encountered his antithesis where small talent is buoyed up by outrageous conceit.

'The superior man is distressed by his want of ability'

Confucius 551-479 BC (33)

Confucius points out the paradox which propels high-achievers forward toward greater heights.

'The eternal problem for the performer is the settling of his own mental equilibrium, the striking of a happy mean between conceit, self-confidence and a sober valuation of his worth.'
'Let us remember when we witness an artist on the platform radiating the most sublime self-assurance that in reality he may be extremely modest and nervous, that he has donned a cloak of self-complacency to disguise his fright. For my part I am aware, when acknowledging applause, that I wear my warmest smile when I know that I have played badly; the smile helps me to walk off the stage and masks my fury. A bad performance haunts an artist for days and days and the memory of it is only erased by a good one. The most vigilant self-criticism is of course necessary, but the time comes when the artist must tell himself he is good or he will go under.' It is a fight.'

Gerald Moore (9)
(Am I Too Loud?)

This quote, by the accompanist, Gerald Moore, perfectly encapsulates the dilemma.

'Something like a nervous dread often takes possession of me while I am on stage in the presence of a large audience.....one can hardly imagine how painful this sensation may be....this sense of uncertainty has often inflicted upon me tortures only to be compared with the Inquisition, while the public listening to me imagines that I am perfectly calm.'

Anton Rubinstein (10)

'The guitar is very curious, I always say the guitar behaves unpredictably because of the influence of it's feminine curves. (Sorry - I know this is politically incorrect - but it's what the man said!)When I go to the concert I am always nervous; then when I begin the concert I am ready to cancel it; but when I have finished the concert, I would like to begin again.'

Andrés Segovia (11)

And you thought *you* had problems! I find these quotations both inspiring and comforting. It is surprising to many people to learn that *great* artists and performers were and are assailed by these feelings of dread and self-doubt. One of the factors which defines their greatness is *how* they react to these doubts. If they are completely banished complacency flourishes and a powerful motivator is lost, but if this doubt gains the upper hand then confidence and further progress will be severely impeded. The trick is to get the *balance* right. This state of equilibrium is difficult to attain, and difficult to maintain, requiring almost constant adjustment. The secret of *success* is how we react to *failure*. There is no doubt that a realistic belief in oneself provides a potent impetus to successful performance, and vice versa. On writing about the sheer *power* of the imagination, the 16th century essayist, **Michel de Montaigne,** made these trenchant observations:

'There are some who from fear anticipate the executioner's hand; and there was one who, when they unbound his eyes so that his pardon might be read to him, was found to be stark dead on the scaffold, slain by no other stroke than that of the imagination.'

Michel de Montaigne 1586 (12)

'Live music performance is an exciting, fragile and unpredictable experience. It demands a blend of strength, love and determination which few possess.'

David Dubal (13)

In my experience of concert giving over some twenty-five years, I have found that no matter how pleased (rarely) or disappointed (frequently) I am concerning the performance it is ,objectively, never as good or as bad as perceived. As a member of an audience I also note that what communicates, above all, is the *spirit* of the performance and not the fine detail. Obviously one has to aim for technical perfection, but for a performer to be convinced a whole concert was appalling because there were a few slips is clearly wrong.

In fact, I remember a very memorable recital at the Wigmore Hall at which I was present and which I very much enjoyed, it was also repertoire with which I was largely familiar. I was convinced the performance was note perfect as well as truly inspiring and musical. When, months later, I heard the concert broadcast

on BBC Radio 3, I was amazed to hear a few obvious errors, but found I had been correct about the event being truly musical and inspiring. This experience taught me a valuable lesson - If the inspiration and spirit of the music, and say 85-95% accuracy, are present, then that concert is a great success and an uplifting event for
the audience (of whom maybe 1 - 3 % will have noticed the errors) and, if the other neccessary factors were present, this will not have marred their enjoyment of the concert as a whole.

I also feel that outstanding performance on any musical instrument can only be achieved through hard and painstaking work. The musician who excels above his colleagues is, generally, the one who has taken more pains. This is also sometimes a surprise to, not only the general public, but also, other musicians, who, also being part of the general public, half-believe outstanding virtuosity and musicality to be innate. This misconception is often fuelled by well-known musicians claiming their practice is minimal, and, indeed, by them trying to make meagre effort a virtue! We all met at school the pupils who claimed they hadn't revised and then came top of the class, believing that a) their peers would think them 'swots' if they admitted they had been up all night revising b) adopting this attitude gave them a 'safety net' if they didn't get good marks c) how much more impressive to appear as a natural genius d) this attitude would also deter would-be competitors who believed themselves inferior.

'The guitar is a jealous mistress, she will not love you if you don't spend the time with her.'

Leo Brouwer (14)

'Two days away from the piano means 'spaghetti fingers.'

Dinu Lipatti (15)

'You can never have sorrow for more than two hours a day when you practise. It brings happiness.'

Andrés Segovia (16)

'It's funny, the more I practise - the luckier I get.'

Gary Player (17)

'Look, I will play the wonderful nocturne of Chopin. The legato thirds seem simple! Ah, if I could only tell you of the years that are behind those thirds. The human mind is peculiar in its method of mastering the movements of the fingers, and to get a great masterpiece so that you have supreme control over it at all times and under all conditions demands a far greater effort than the ordinary non-professional music-lover can imagine.'

Vladimir de Pachmann (18)

'We guitarists - or any serious musicians - need the stern discipline of life-long practice, many years of self-denial. Many hours and weeks polishing a single passage, burnishing it to bring out its true sparkle. The creation of beautiful imagery demands the cares of gestation and the pains of childbirth.'

Andrés Segovia (19)

So regular practice is essential. I do feel, however, that those lucky enough to have been the recipients of top quality tuition from a very early age probably need to do less *technical* work than those who haven't been so lucky. Of course one doesn't have to have an instrument in one's hands to practise , and much valuable work can be done away from the instrument, particularly in the field of memorization. I personally derive great benefit from not only 'playing' a piece mentally and hearing the sound and timbre of the notes, but also in imagining a successful concert scenario. Even when practising with the instrument I feel that it is basically an intellectual rather than physical exercise.

'...create a future history - it's about seeing yourself achieving your objectives and making them happen.'

Judi James (20) (Authoress of 'Body Talk')

'One plays the piano with one's mind not one's fingers.'

Glenn Gould (21)

'I always practise the technically difficult passages first - separately and slowly - so that I learn to control and phrase them. One must resist the temptation to try out the right tempo until one has perfect control at the slower tempo. I never play such passages mechanically with the intention of adding the phrasing later. A technically difficult passage needs to be played more slowly until you learn to control it - but with the right musical expression. To separate the technical from the expressive side in music is like separating the body from the soul.'

Daniel Barenboim (22)

Barenboim's comments on *slow* practise are so true. We are all impatient to play the piece up to tempo, or beyond, but, unless the firm technical and musical foundation has been laid, we will not gain mastery over the music. The repetition of 'hit and miss' renditions only serve to ingrain the bad technical habits further. However, these undesirable technical traits can be removed, and it is easier to change one's method of playing than generally thought. I often use the example of driving an unfamiliar car - it all feels strange and alien when we sit behind a new wheel because it is different from the vehicle we are used to, however, we very quickly adapt to the new machine, (even if it has a radical difference like having the steering wheel on the other side) and, in a very short space of time, we have become at ease with our new driving environment. When we then return to the car we have been driving for years, it feels strangely odd and different. In driving we also have the extra incentive, that our lives could depend on our coming to successful terms with the new vehicle! I have certainly found these sometimes drastic changes very possible to achieve when related to guitar playing, it is just a case of remembering different 'motor' (no pun intended) actions and feelings.

Of course, one never arrives at the point when one can say, 'O.K. That's it, I can now play.' - It's a lifetime's work for anyone whoever they are, and one's ideals are often subtly changing. Listening to old recordings of oneself dramatically illustrates one's changing musical sensibilities, I am often appalled by my own efforts! I now, as a matter of course, constantly record myself and find this very useful and instructive to my learning and evolving processes and strongly recommend the regular use of a tape recorder when practising, it can give great insights into one's playing and even though it sometimes teaches rather painful lessons, it pays huge dividends. The great Canadian pianist **Glenn Gould (23)** said: *'The tape recorder is the finest teacher.'* and he should know as he abandoned his concert career, in his early thirties, to concentrate exclusively on recording until his death aged 51.

Pupils of all standards all, with the rarest of exceptions, have elements in their playing which can be improved. They must not be daunted by trying some very different approaches, as these can often achieve dramatic results.

Many pupils have asked me over the years, 'How much practice should I do per day, and how much time should I devote to what?'

The most important fact of the matter is that it is, of course *quality* and not *quantity* that is paramount. Trying to give a more specific answer to the question I must say that I would, generally, practise no more than one hour at a time, and probably, the ideal is rather less than that. It is a pointless exercise to practise without concentration and attention, and these disciplines can only be sustained for a limited period. Over an average day I would hope altogether to practise at least five hours. As to how this is broken down, I would say about half the time on mainly *technical* work, and the other half on the *musical* aspects, (i.e. learning new repertoire, maintaining established repertoire etc.). But remember Barenboim's quote, and that it is difficult, if not impossible, to totally separate the two. I have found it absolutely vital to work on the *specific* problem in hand itself (say a difficult scale passage), rather than practising many different scales in the hope that the problem passage will become easier. Each problem area in the music is unique both in itself and in the context in which it occurs and needs to be solved with a *flexible* and *individual* approach. Therefore, if studying for example the *'Concierto de Aranjuez'* by **Rodrigo**, (a work which abounds with scale passages) it is not enough to merely practise a lot of scales, the *specific* passages must be addressed, and quite often, different solutions can be, and have to be, found to each technical problem. These solutions must then be practised diligently and intelligently until they can be executed with ease.

Having a routine or format to the practice time is helpful. Although I wouldn't recommend Eric Satie's approach:

'A musician must organise his life. Here is an exact timetable of my daily activities. Get up: 7.18 a.m; be inspired: 10.23 to 11.47 a.m. I take lunch at 12.11 p.m. and leave the table at 12.14 p.m.'

Eric Satie (24)(from 'Memories of an Amnesiac')

I strongly recommend reading and re-reading every possible tutor and manual on playing and technique. (I have also found value in books on *different* instruments, particularly violin and piano). There are, very often, common principles to playing *any* instrument. Everyone has slightly (and sometimes radically) different ideas and one writer's explanation, on a given subject, may suddenly 'click' and provide an illuminating insight into a previously misunderstood area.

If I have an hour to practise, I sometimes take four problematic passages and practise each for fifteen minutes, this rotation helps to keep the concentration focused on the task in hand. If you have practised effectively, you will certainly feel it the next day. Remember to use a minimum of force to produce the note and that volume and velocity are often inversely related:

'To produce a large sound, the fingers should release the string with velocity and weight (not strength and force).'

Pepe Romero (25)

'Police your fingers so that they do not exceed the necessary force for the desired sound.'

Gaspar Sanz (26)

'Do not insert the fingers too deeply into the strings.'

Celedonio Romero (27)

One of the most important lessons I have learnt is to develop a creative approach to fingering, be flexible and resourceful i.e. If one fingering isn't working think of an alternative, and don't slavishly follow the fingering suggested on the page, it is, after all, just one person's solution. We all have different strengths and weaknesses and one person may play with ease what, for another, would be highly difficult. However, *that* person could find *another* equally valid solution to a technical riddle. Personally, my fingering of the same passages changes frequently - sometimes just before a concert (with varying degrees of success!), but one shouldn't be frightened of experimentation. After every performance I usually think - *'Right - back to the drawing board. This worked, that didn't, maybe this might.....'* The thing about the guitar is that there are so many different permutations of fingerings, sounds and phrasings available to the player, and playing is a *continual* learning process.

'One should not only overcome a technical problem, but one must surpass it'.

'You must know the work so well that if you are awakened at 4 'oclock in the morning and told to play a concerto for a conductor - you can do it instantly and without complaint. He (Martin Krause - his teacher) *taught me not to be too finicky about conditions.'*

Claudio Arrau (28)

'An amateur practises to get it right - a professional practises so he can't get it wrong.'

Anon.

'The performing violinist continually reviews the hours, days and weeks preceding a performance, charting the many elements that will release his potential - or put a brake on it. He knows that when his body is exercised, his blood circulating, his stomach light, his mind clear, the music ringing in his heart, his violin clean and polished, it's strings in good order, the bow hair full and evenly spread, then -but then only- he is in command. But neglect of the least of these elements must gnaw his conscience. The audience, even the critic, may not suspect his troubled conscience, or may ascribe a blemish to an irrelevant cause, all unaware of the player's silent admission of insufficiency, his self-disgust, his begging to be given another chance. Even if no fault is noted, the audience's plaudits, their stamping and standing, are of no comfort to him then.'

Yehudi Menuhin (29)

For the week preceding the concert, I play through the programme in it's entirety at least once , and often twice, a day. I isolate particularly difficult sections and practise them *slowly*, sometimes changing the fingering if I find a better one, and, as usual, I practise an array of technical exercises, (all of which feature in the preceding chapters). It is very important, during practice, to be aware of any bodily tensions, however slight, which will, under the strain of live performance, be magnified at least tenfold. If one identifies and addresses them in the practice room, they are less likely to surface in the concert hall. Facial tension is particularly undesirable as it sends the wrong signals to the entire body. Try to remain facially impassive even when playing the most demanding sections of music. Check this in the mirror or, better still record your performance on video. The feet and legs are also a crucial area as they form the foundations of posture and tensions in these areas again tend to communicate to the rest of the body.

I have found recently, with the help and instruction of Prof. Carola Grindea, it is helpful, during practice and performance, to exhale very slowly through the mouth. This has a very beneficial calming and relaxing effect and I wholeheartedly recommend the book, *'Tensions in the Performance of Music'* (Kahn & Averill, London), which she has edited and contributed a chapter.

On the day of the concert, if it is within driving distance, I normally run through the programme, do a few technical exercises, and arrive at the venue about an hour before the performance. Having played for a short time in the hall itself, I simply warm up in the dressing room by playing technical exercises, very seldom do I play through any of the pieces in the recital. If on an extended tour where there is a daily or nightly, or sometimes both, performance, I feel less need to practise for huge amounts of time. I've found that one concert is worth about ten hours of practice, and I usually feel good (playing-wise), the next day.

It is very important to listen to a wide range of music played on different instruments, and not to be focussed solely on the guitar and it's repertoire, and, indeed, to draw inspiration and nourishment from the other branches of the arts, we must remind ourselves what the great Paraguayan guitarist and composer **Agustín Barrios** (30) said on this subject:

' One cannot become a guitarist if he has not bathed in the fountain of culture.'

I remember my own experience of attending series after series of international string quartet concerts in my home town, (these events, sadly, no longer occur). From these concerts I developed a real appreciation and love of chamber music, which certainly exerted a powerful influence on my guitar playing. I also listened widely to orchestral music and the solo piano, developing a particular fondness for Bach, Beethoven, Mozart, Bartok and Scarlatti. This wider listening experience gives a valuable perspective on the 'guitar' pieces of whatever era we are studying. These pieces, after all, were not created in a vacuum and ideas for transcriptions may also very well occur to us when we explore other instruments' repertoires. The interpretative insights which are gleaned as a direct result of this process are absolutely invaluable. As a teacher I have often found the difference between a coherent and incoherent reading of a particular piece is almost always directly proportionate to a student's general background listening experience.

It is impossible to overestimate the importance of going to hear and see as many first- class players as possible, and this is one of the most exciting and inspiring ways to learn, but hearing even a poor player can be inspirational:

'There may be some persons of my temperament who learn more by avoidance than by imitation, and by shunning rather than by following. It was this sort of teaching that the elder Cato had in mind when he said that wise men have more to learn from fools than fools from wise men; and that ancient player on the lyre also, who, according to Pausanias's story, was in the habit of making his pupils go and listen to a wretched strummer who lived across the way, where they might learn to hate his discords and false measures.'

Michel de Montaigne (1586) (31)

It is important not to forget one's original inspirations and to refer back to them often. They are, after all, the reason you play, and generally, I am willing to bet, you will still find them inspiring. In my case, for exponents of duo guitar, the Abreu Brothers (Sergio & Eduardo) were a revelation (and still are!), for solo (and my first ever experience of the classical guitar) it must be Andres Segovia's account of the 'Chaconne' by J.S.Bach which I immediately tried to play!...also the recordings of Los Romeros and Sabicas continue to inspire. Listen and luxuriate in your favourite recordings and let them fuel your enthusiasm. Although there are now many fine players of the guitar worldwide it is still, unfortunately, relatively rare to get the chance to see and hear them (especially in a concerto or ensemble context). If you *do* get the chance - make sure you take it and hear them live - it's a great inspiration and worth a million CDs!

Finally, I would like to emphasise the importance to the guitarist of playing with other musicians. The combination of *two* guitars, in my opinion, is one of the most effective and enjoyable, but, of course, I am biased! The guitar combines particularly well with the violin, the voice, the flute, the mandolin, the recorder, the oboe and with all manner of small chamber ensembles and there is much more repertoire in these areas than often realised. When you play in these various ensembles, open your head to the full musical picture, listen to the whole of the music and not just *your* part. It will greatly increase your delight in playing and will help you to play your part more effectively and musically.

Good luck and great enjoyment from your playing.

✳ ▲ ✹ ✻ ✺ ▲ ✳

Robin Hill 1999

V.
APPENDIX

Further pieces for study

Esercizio No. 3

to Mario Gangi

Robin Hill

Guitar I, Guitar II

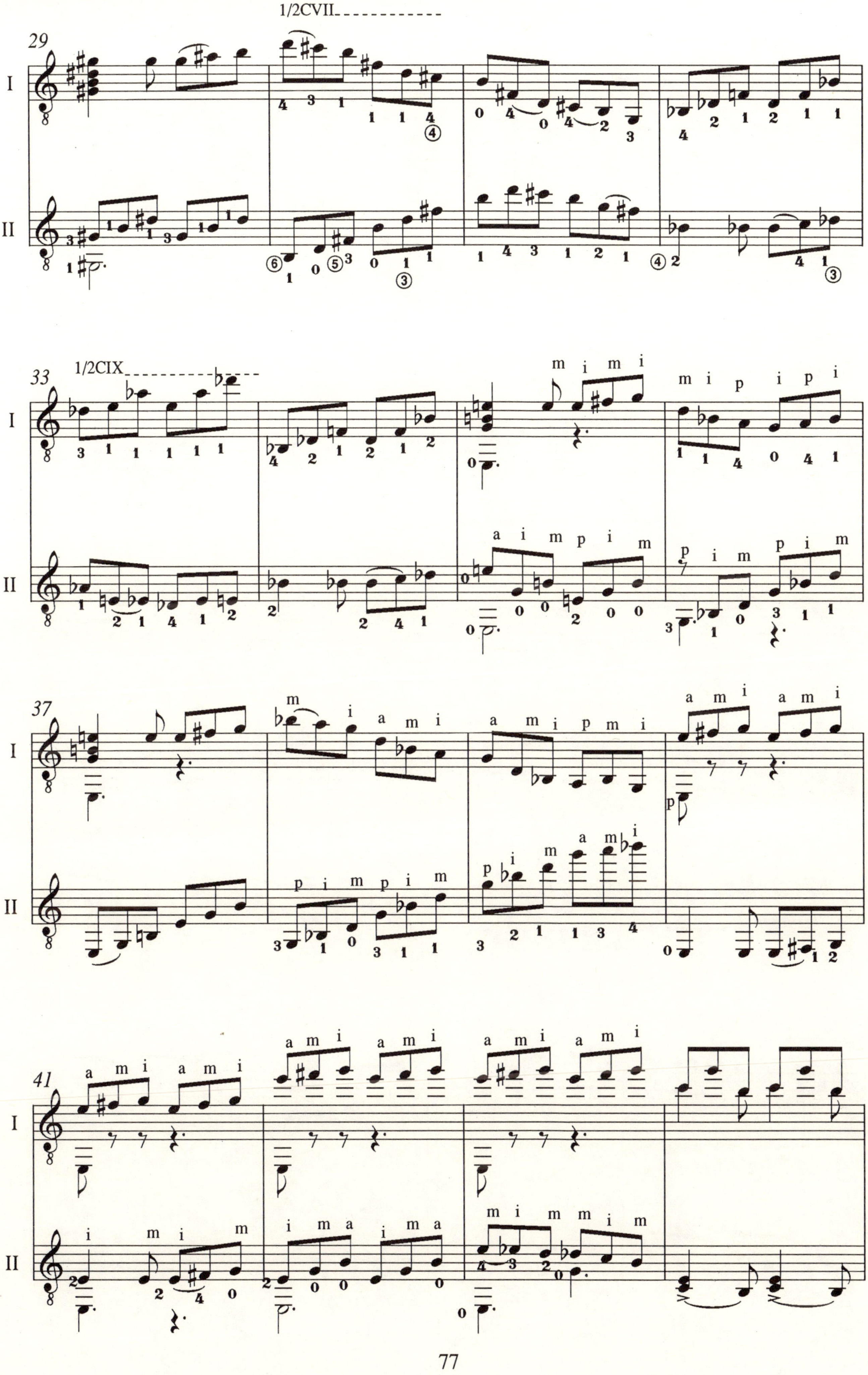
1/2CVII
1/2CIX
I
II
29
33
37
41

Guitar I, Guitar II

Guitar I, Guitar II

Guitar I, Guitar II

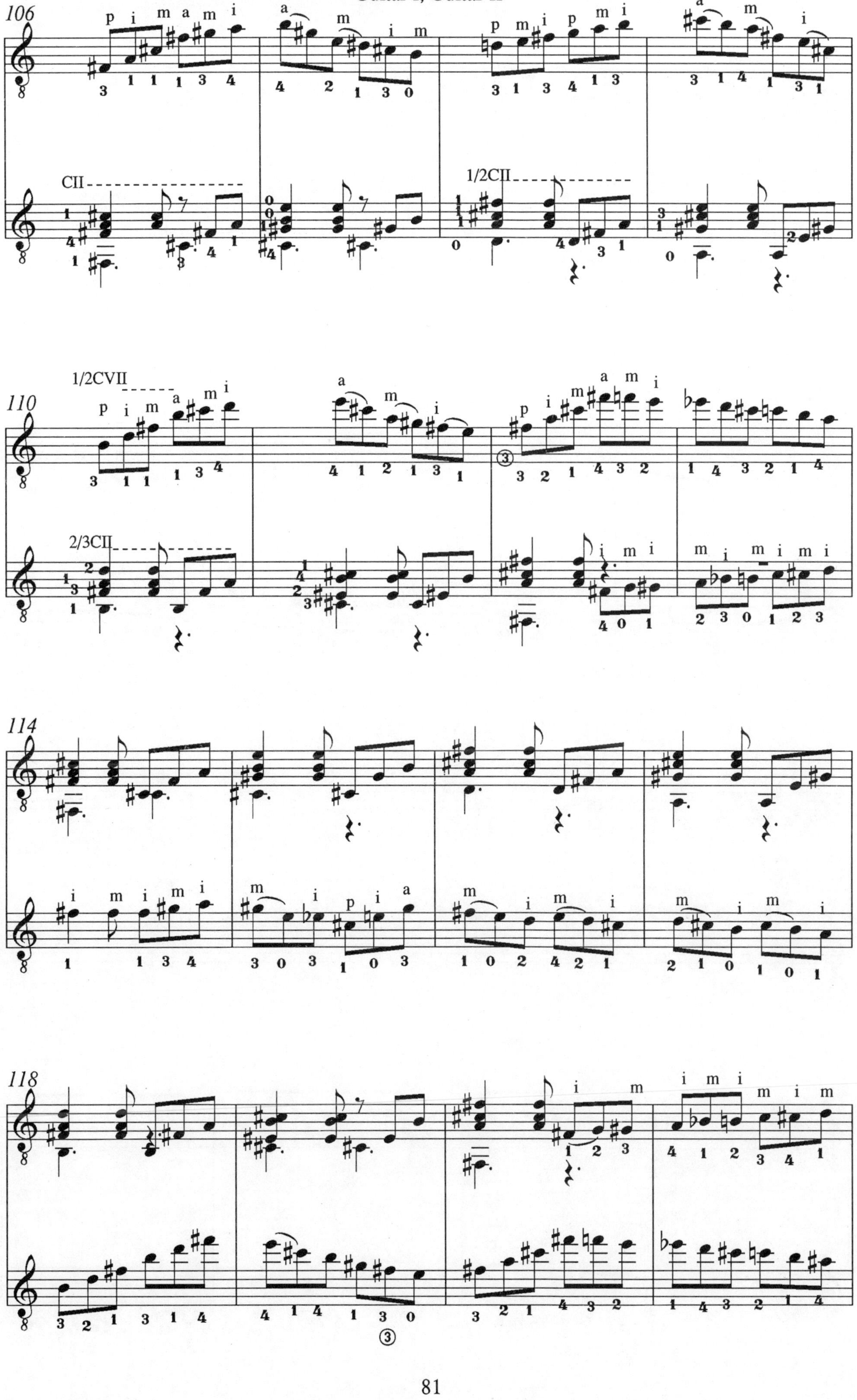
106
I
II
CII
1/2CII
110
1/2CVII
2/3CII
114
118

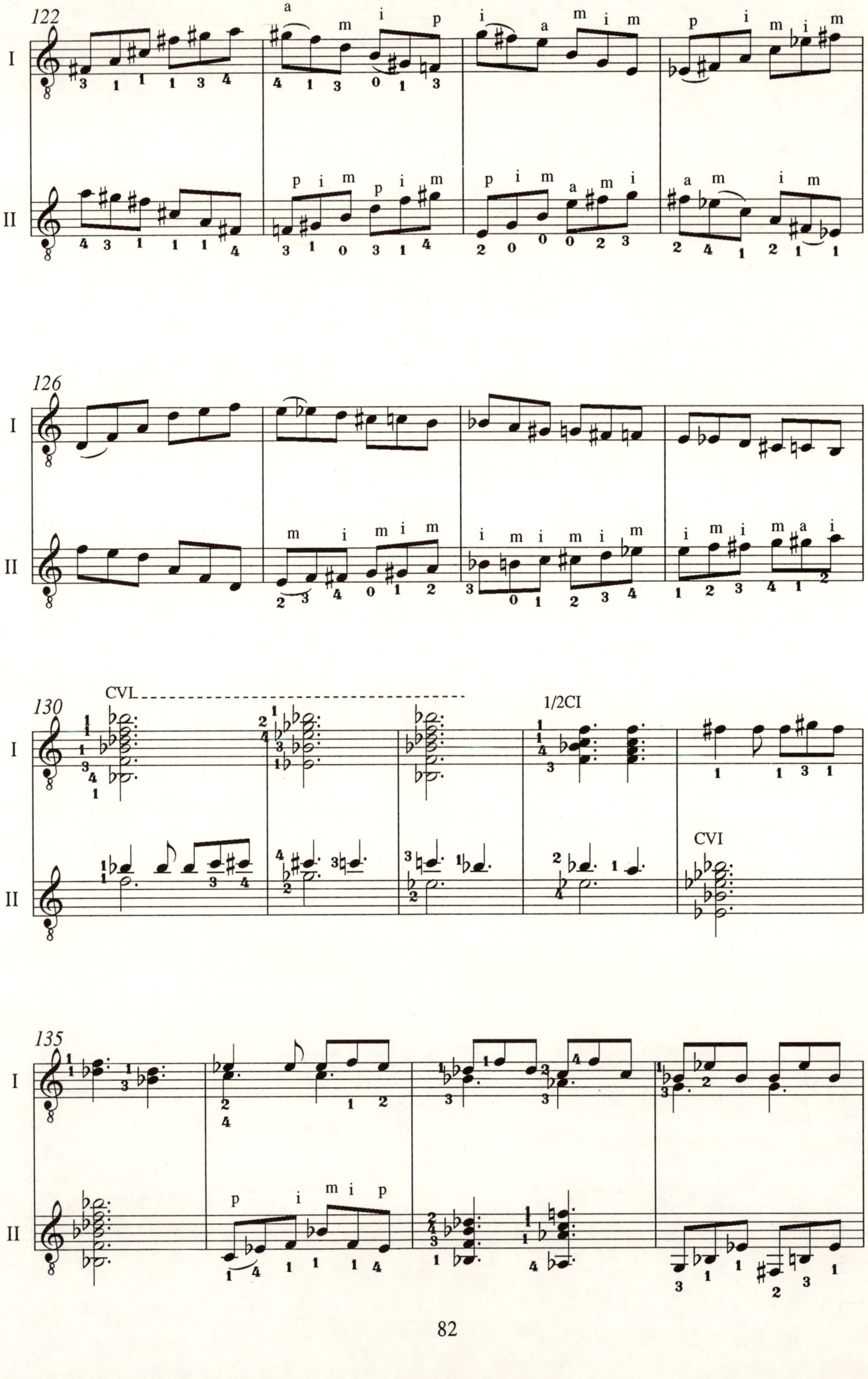
122
I
II
126
I
II
130
CVI
1/2CI
CVI
I
II
135
I
II

Guitar I, Guitar II

100 Exercises for Right Hand

Robin Hill

*These exercises were inspired by Mauro Giuliani's 120 right hand exercises
which, along with his left hand exercises, I wholeheartedly recommend for daily practice.*

(All exercises should be practised firstly without bass)

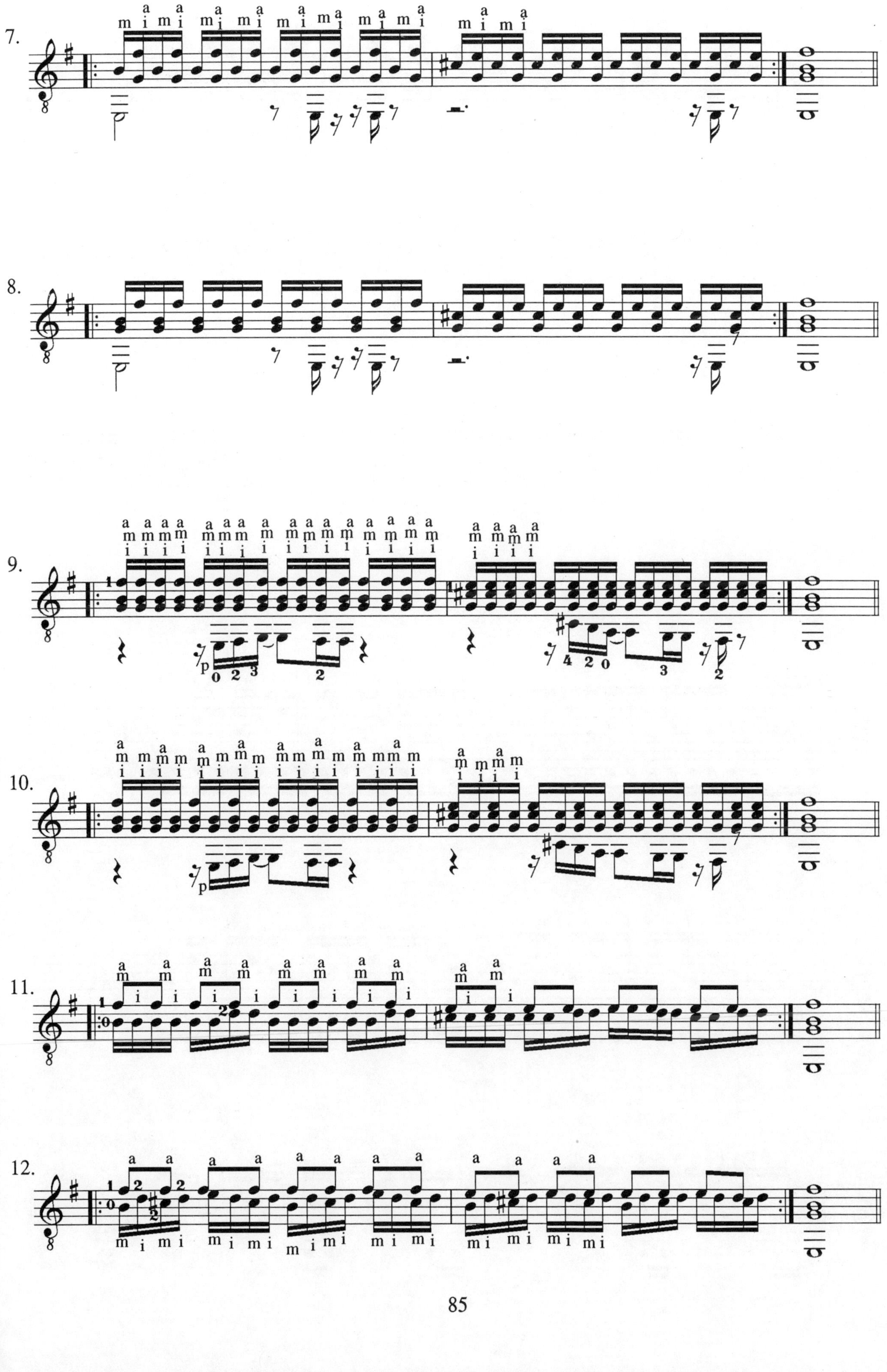
7.
8.
9.
10.
11.
12.

13.

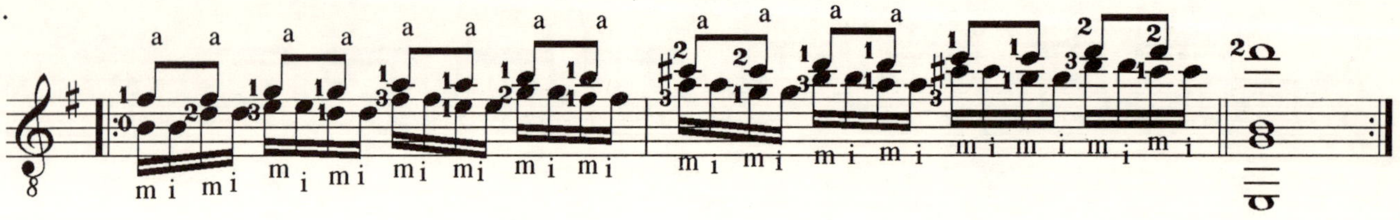

14.

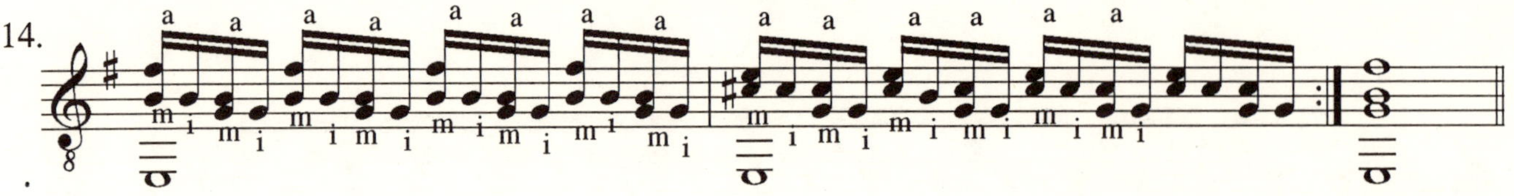

15.

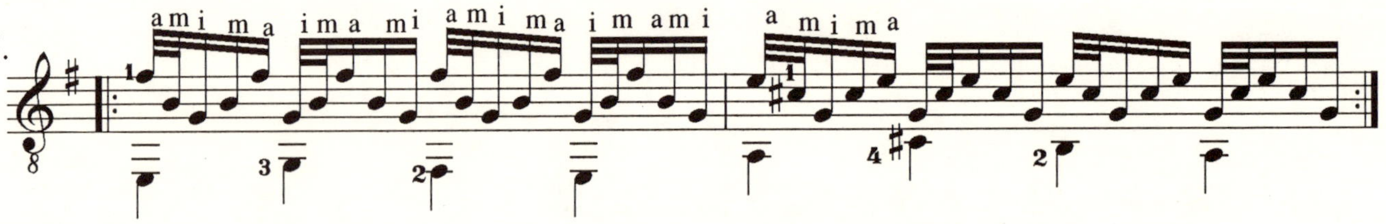

16.

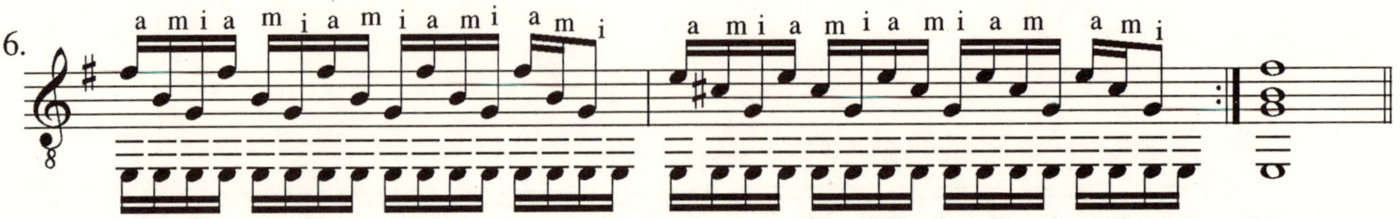

17.

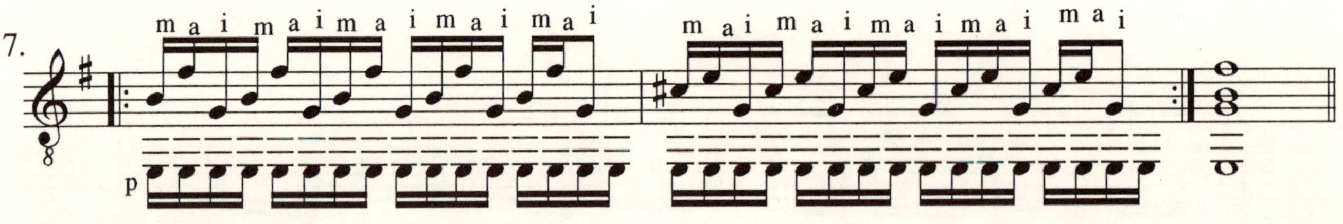

18.

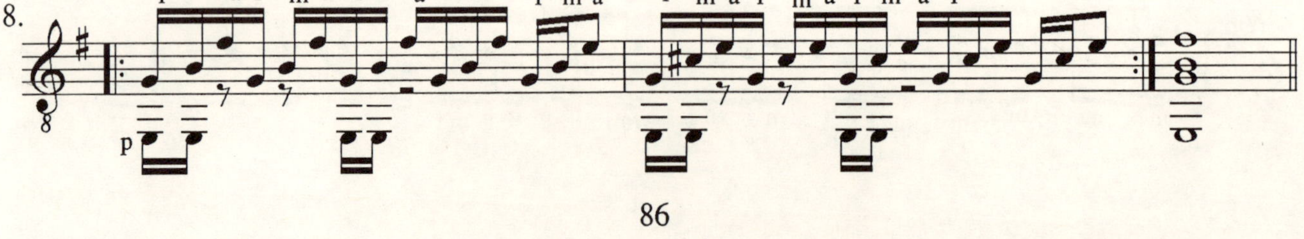

19.

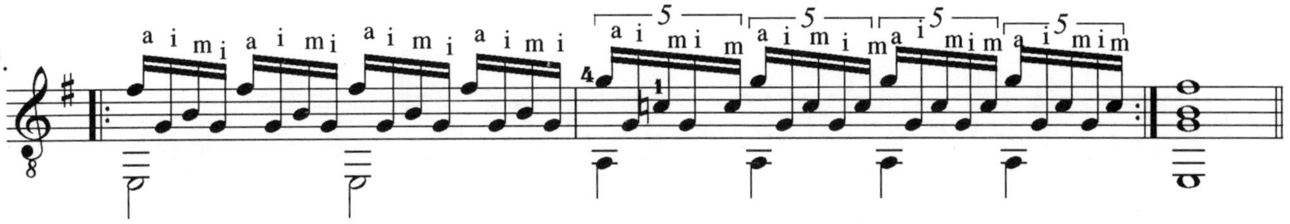

20.

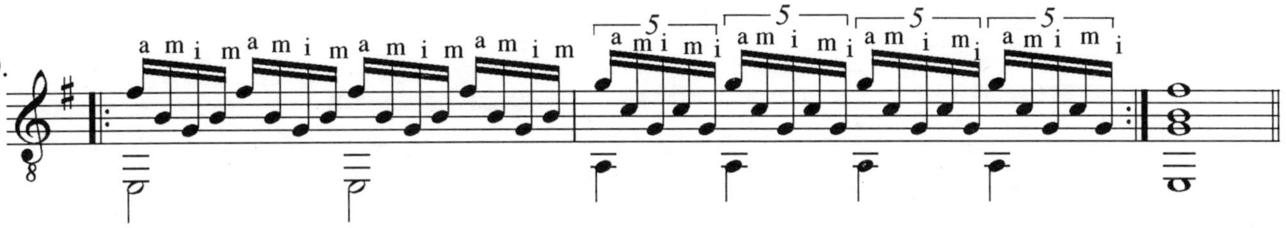

21.

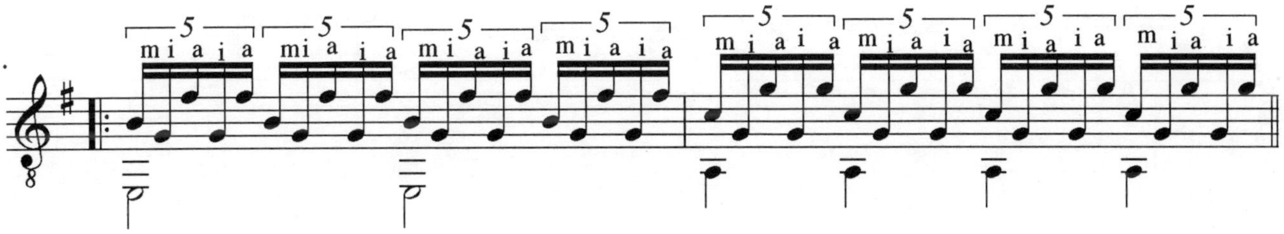

22.

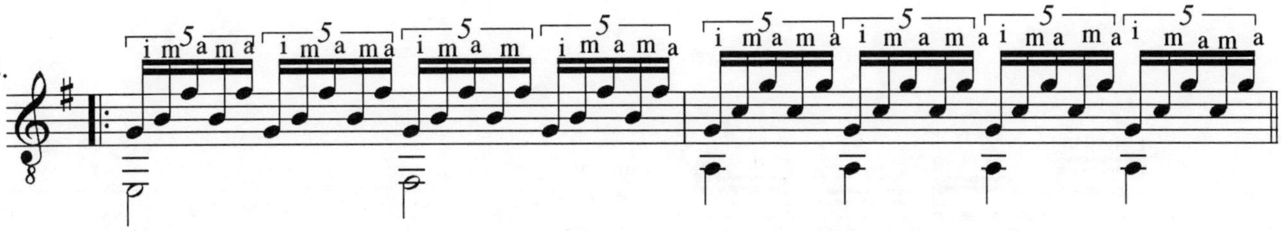

23.

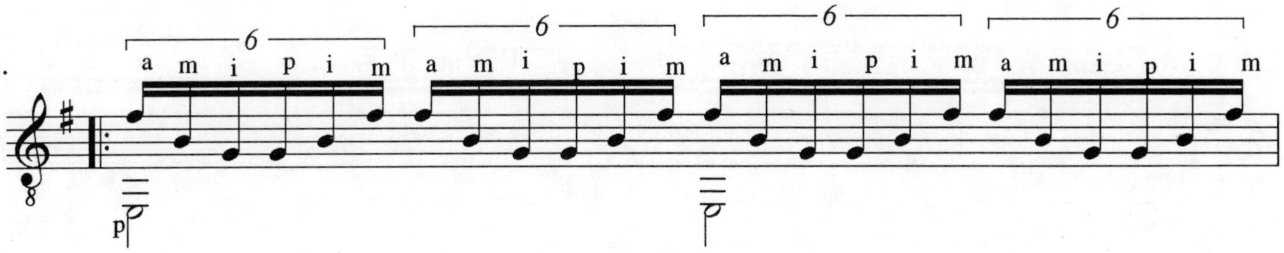

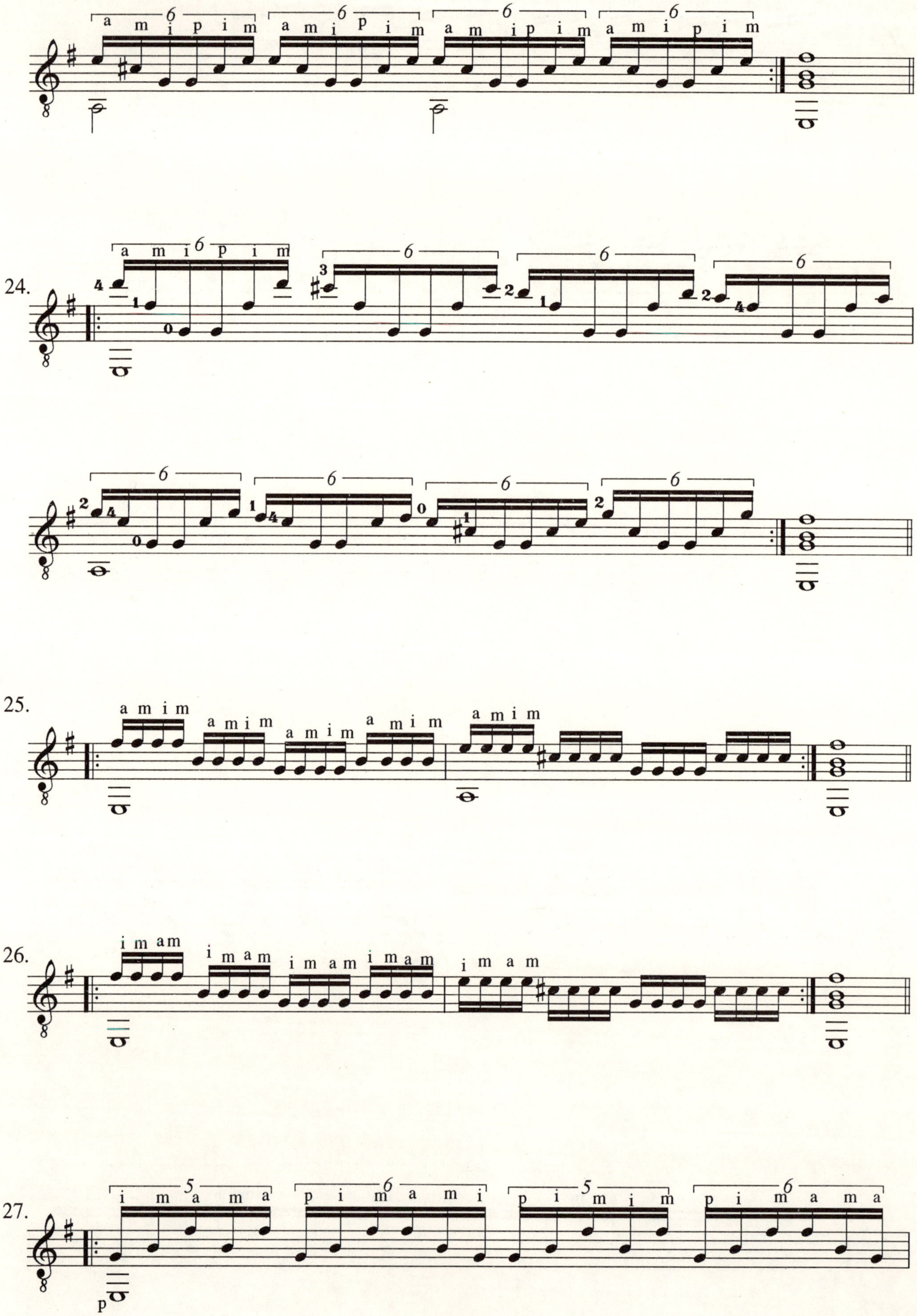
24.
25.
26.
27.

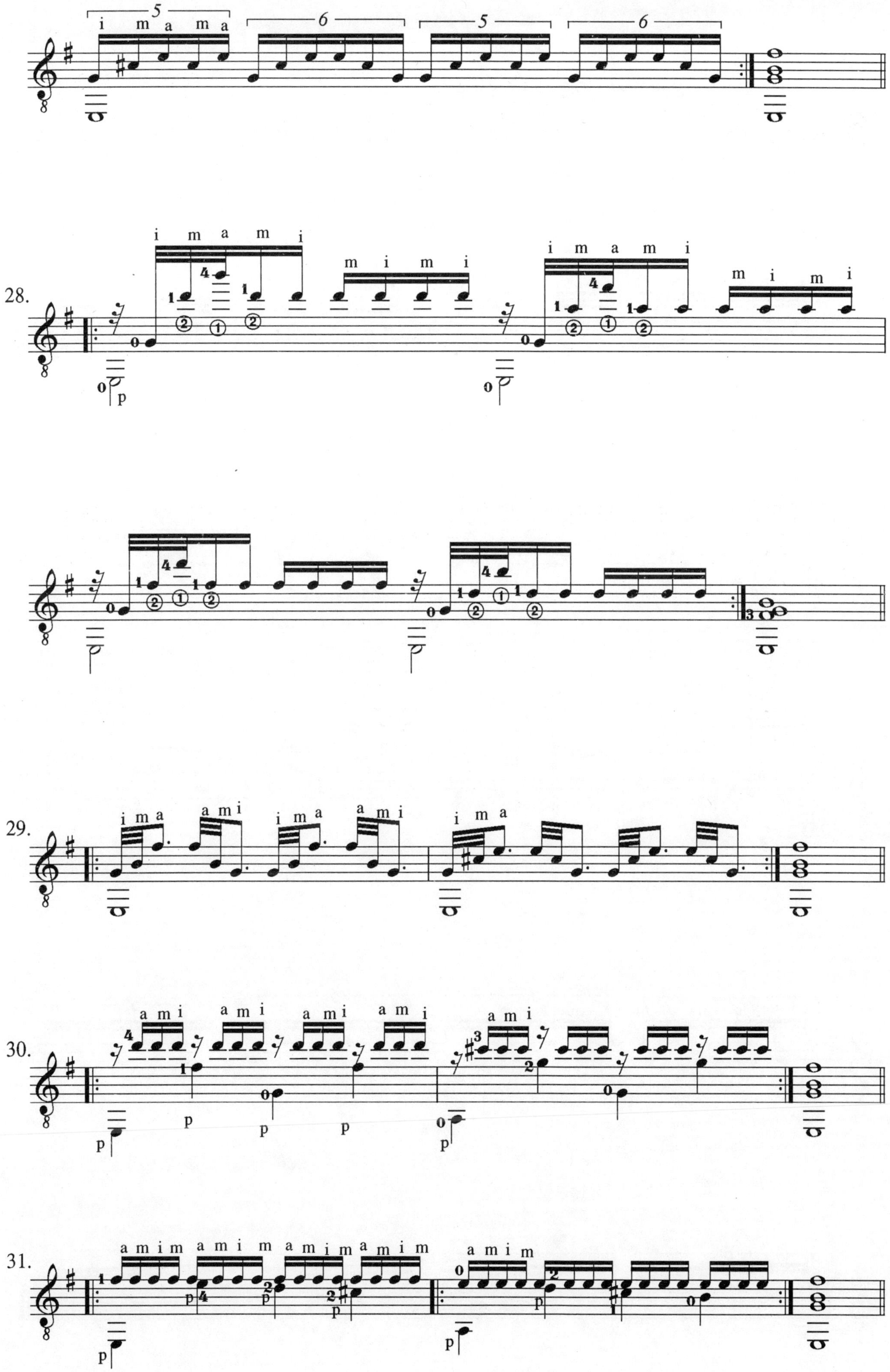
28.
29.
30.
31.

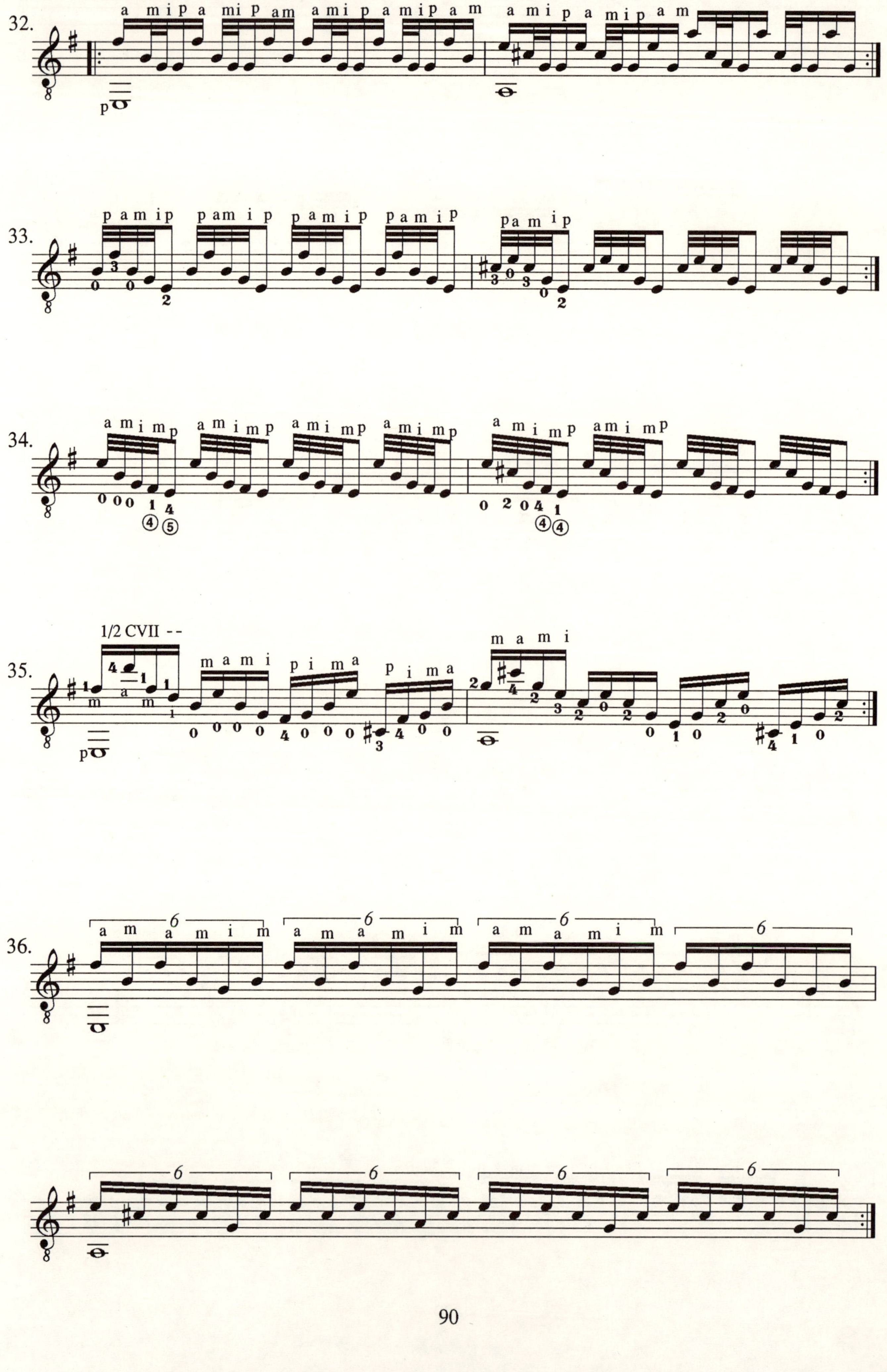
32.
33.
34.
35.
1/2 CVII - -
36.

37.

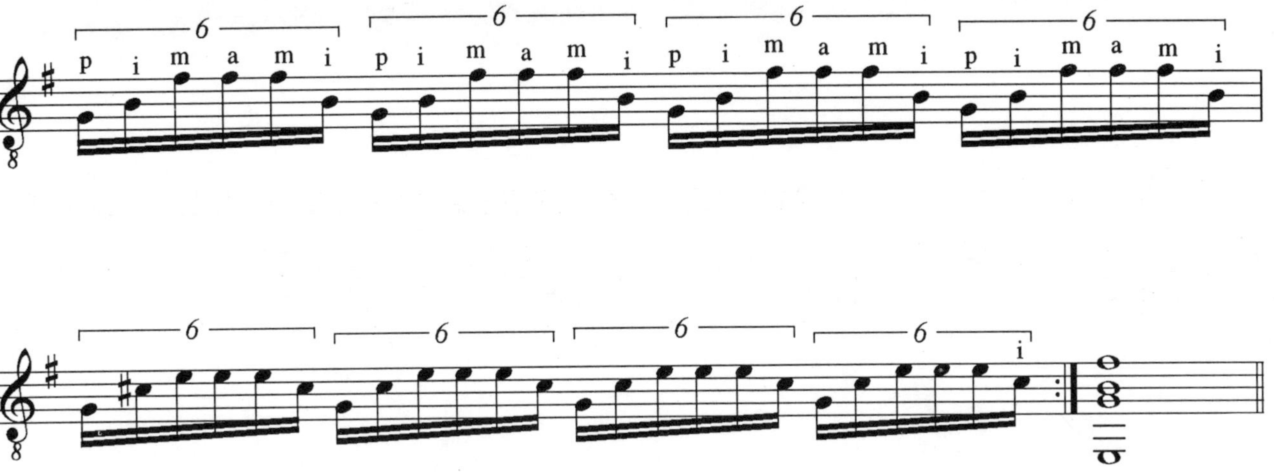
p i m a m i p i m a m i p i m a m i p i m a m i
6 6 6 6
6 6 6 6
i

38.

a m i a m i a m i a m i a m i a m i a m i a m i
6 6 6 6
6 6 6 6

39.

p i m a m p i m a m p i m a m p i m a m p i m a m
5 5 5 5 5 5 5 5

40.

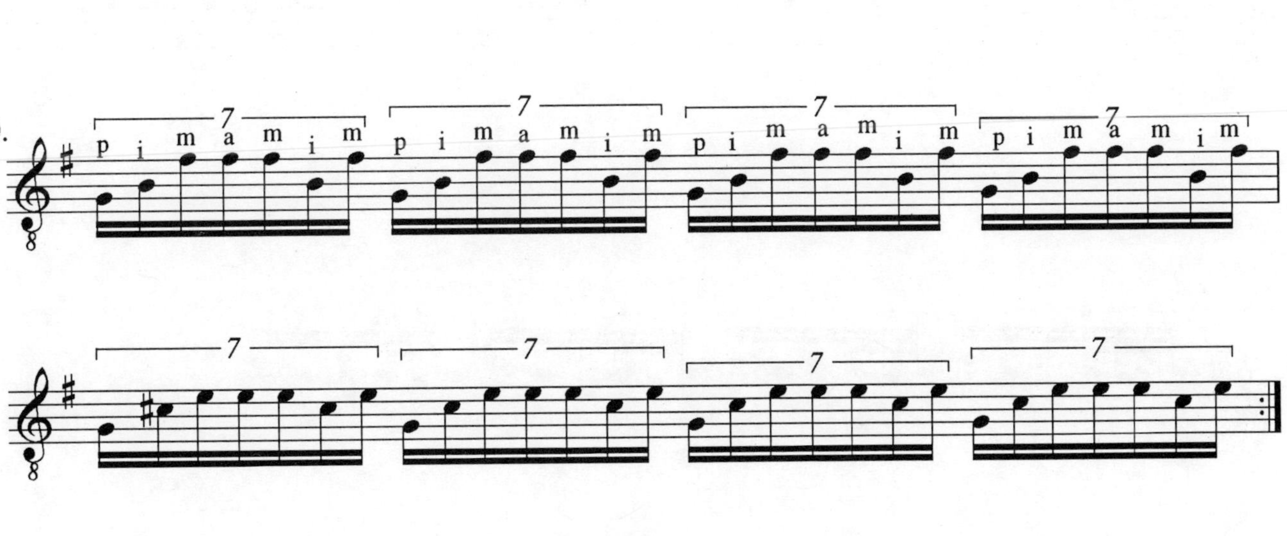
p i m a m i m p i m a m i m p i m a m i m p i m a m i m
7 7 7 7
7 7 7 7

92

44.
i a i m a m i a i m a
p
45.
a i m p m a i m p m a i m p m a i m p m
p
46.
a i m i a i m i a i m i a i m i a i m i a i m i
p

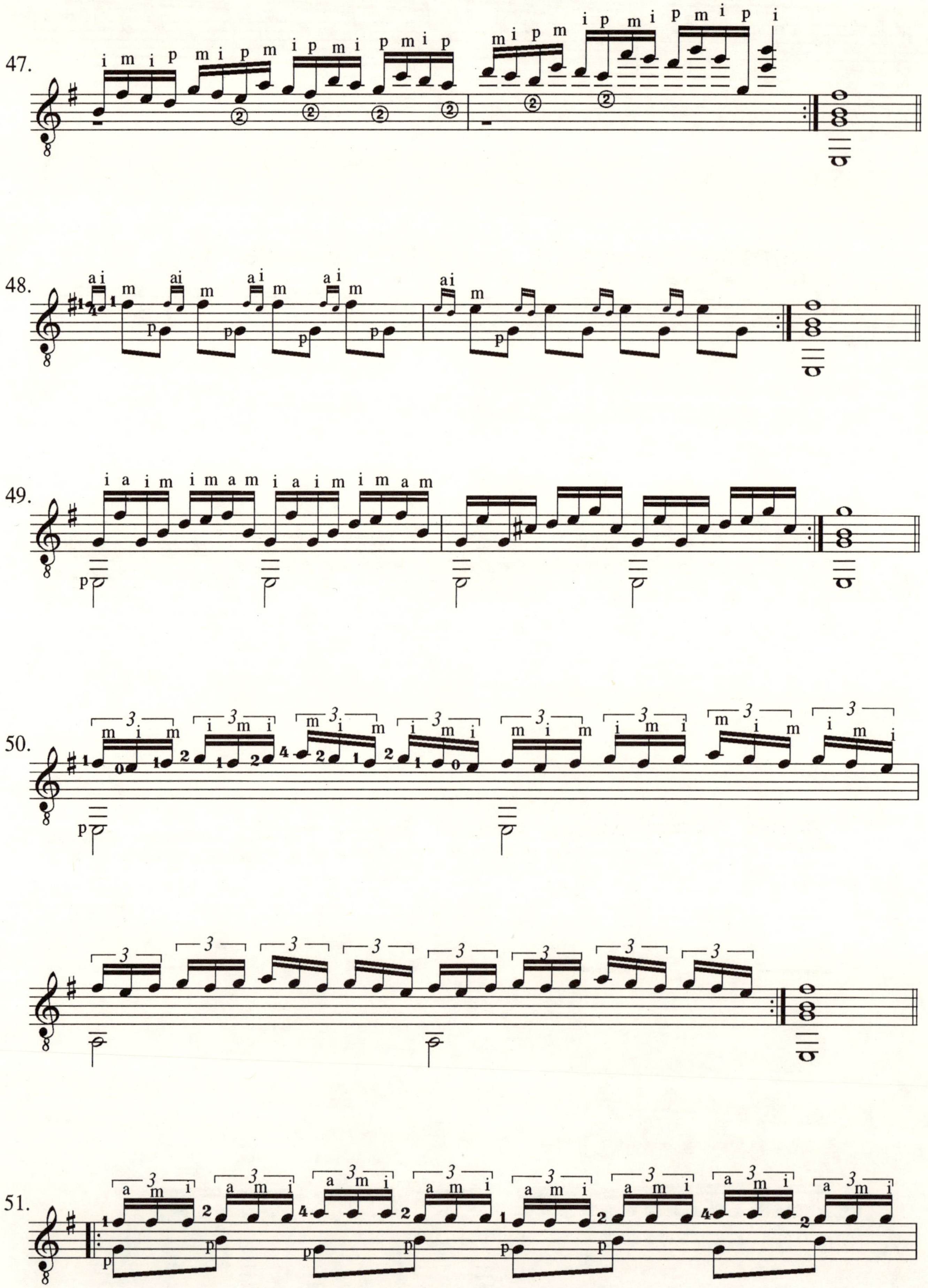
47.
48.
49.
50.
51.

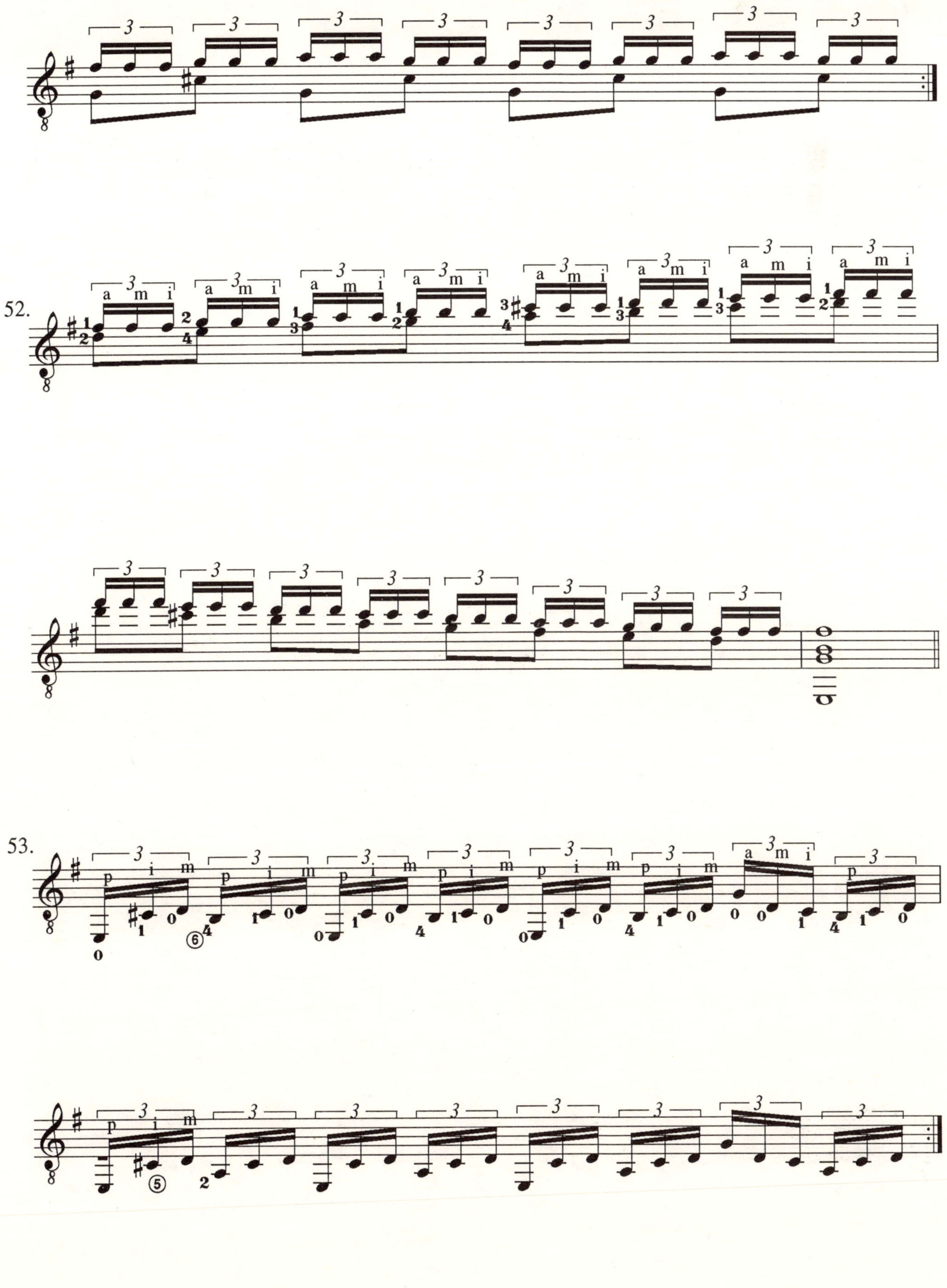
52.
53.
54.

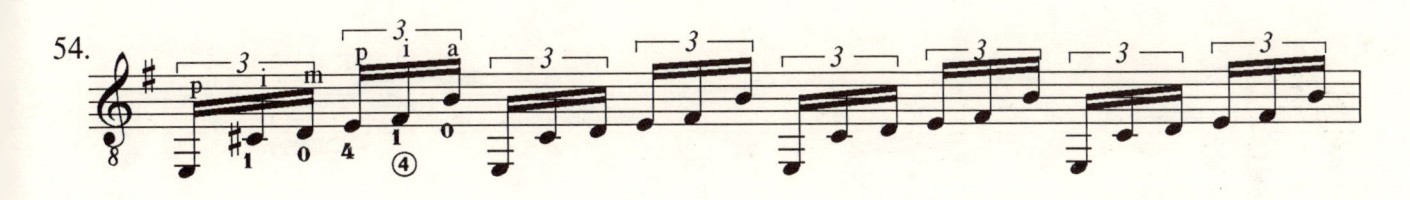

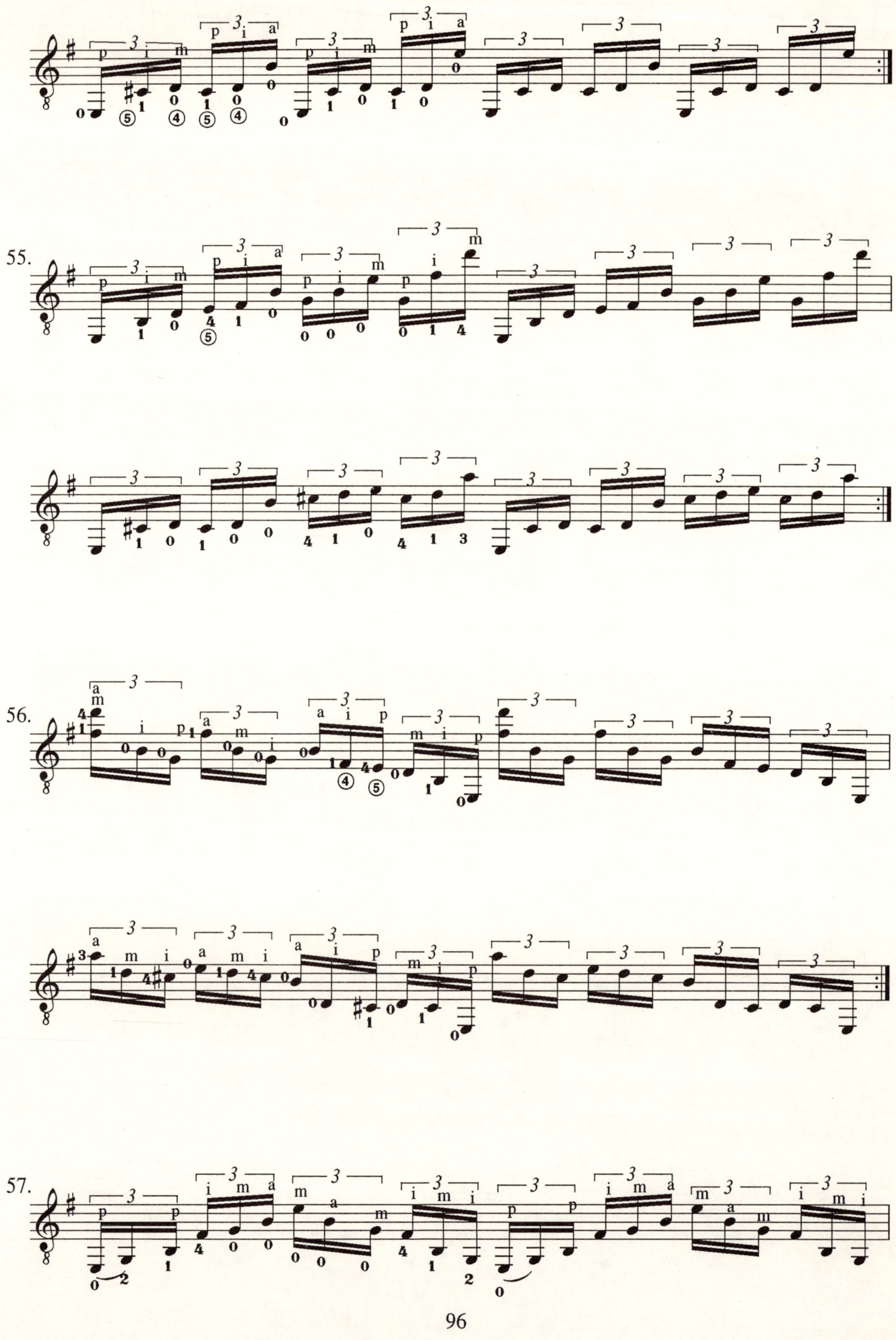
55.
56.
57.

97

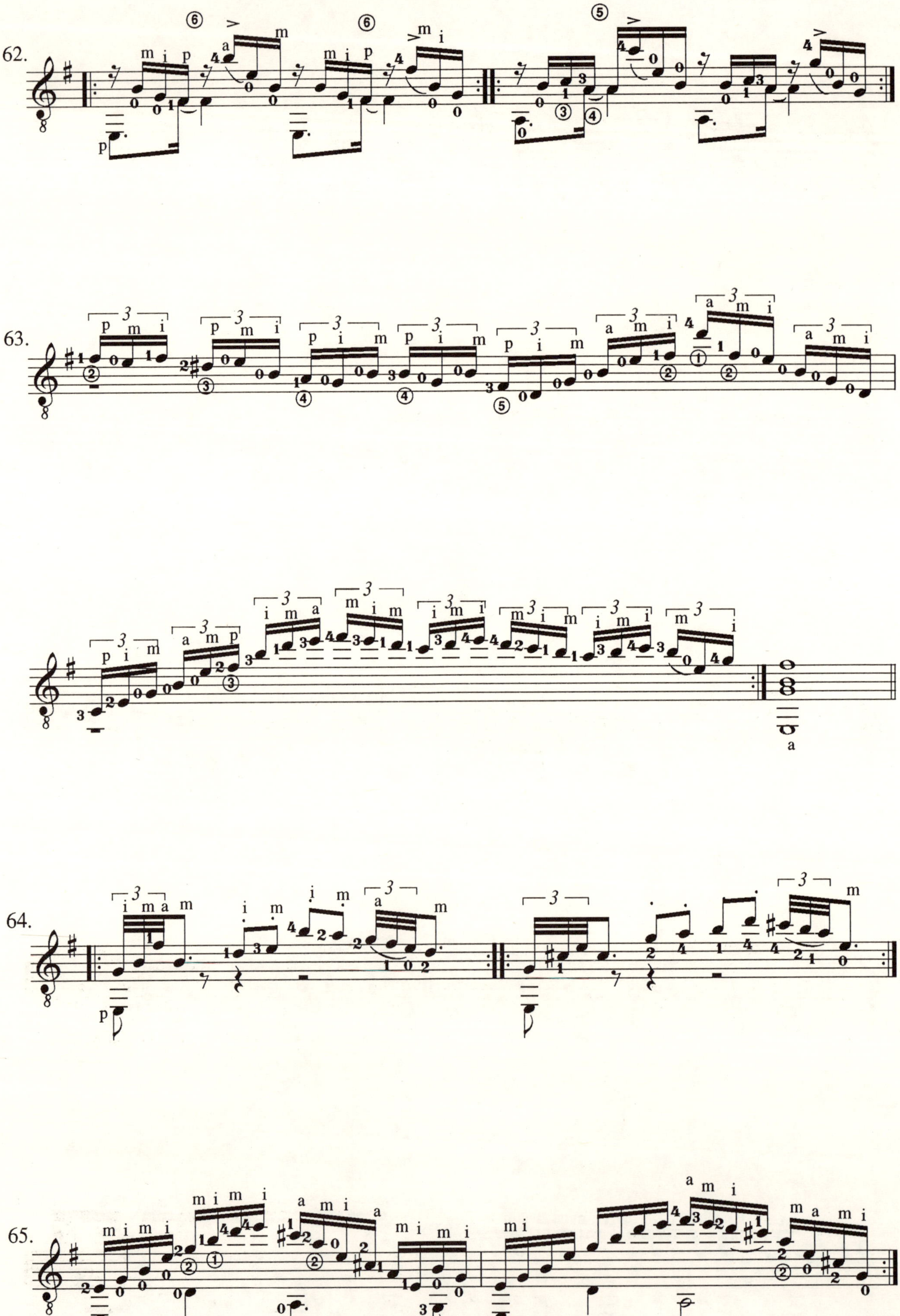
62.
63.
64.
65.

99

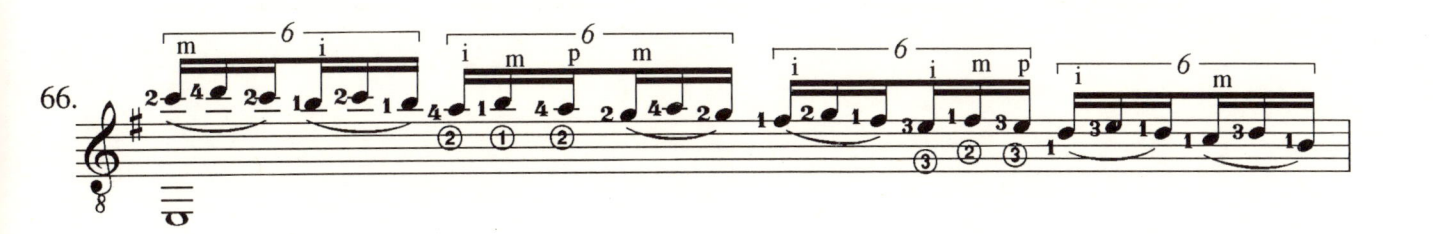

100

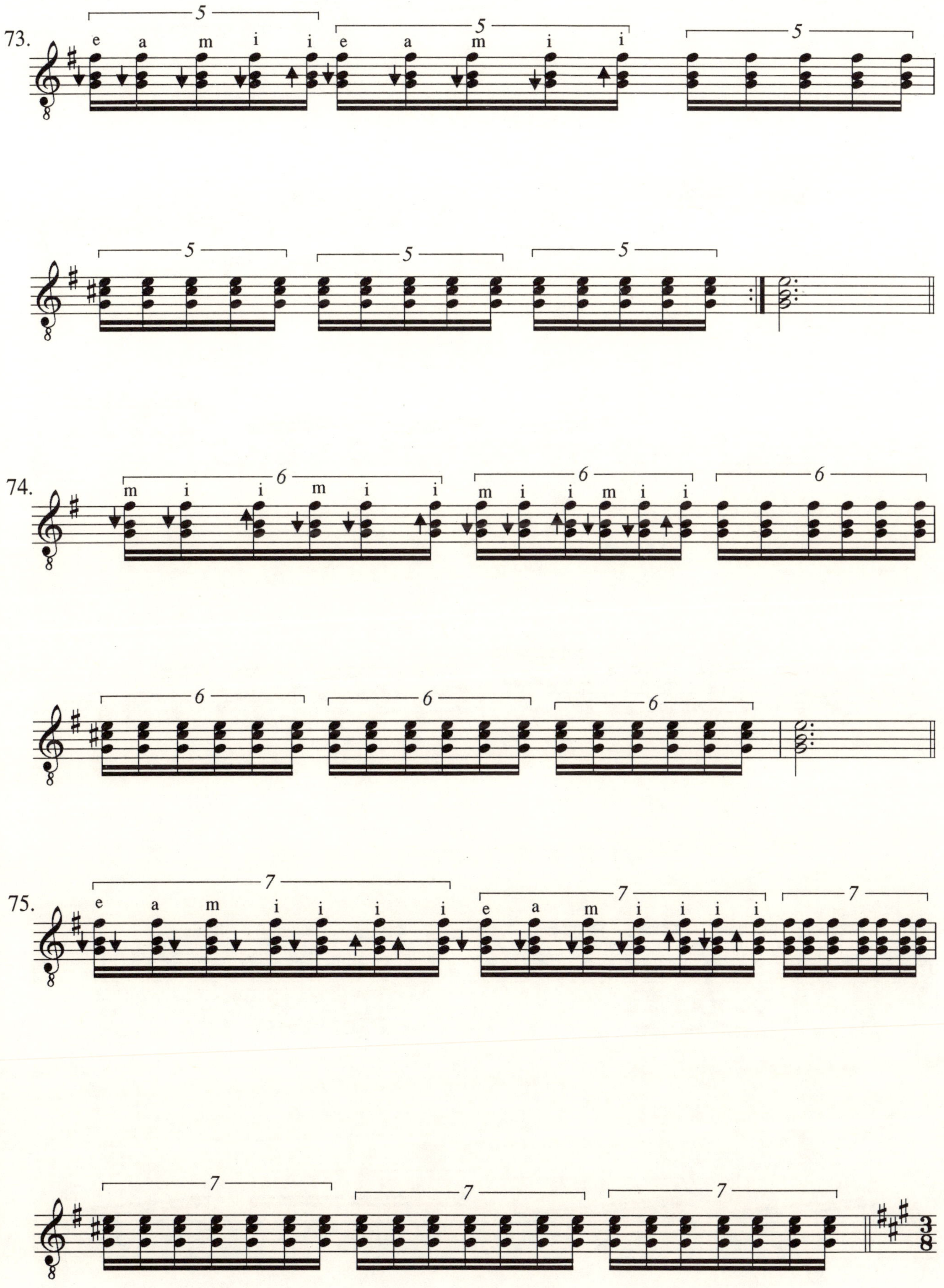
73.
e a m i i e a m i i
5
74.
m i i m i i m i i m i i
6
75.
e a m i i i i e a m i i i i
7

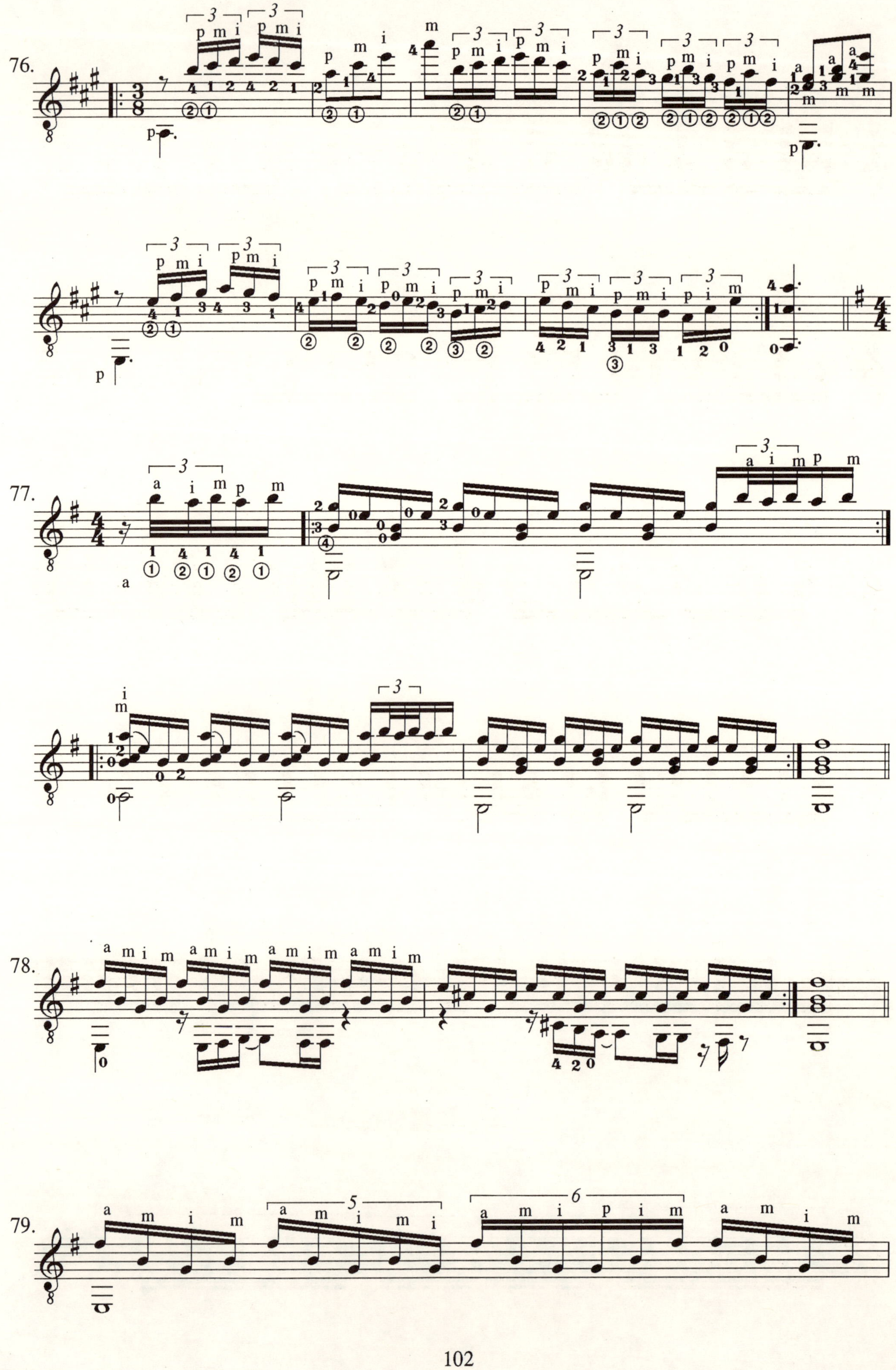
76.
77.
78.
79.

103

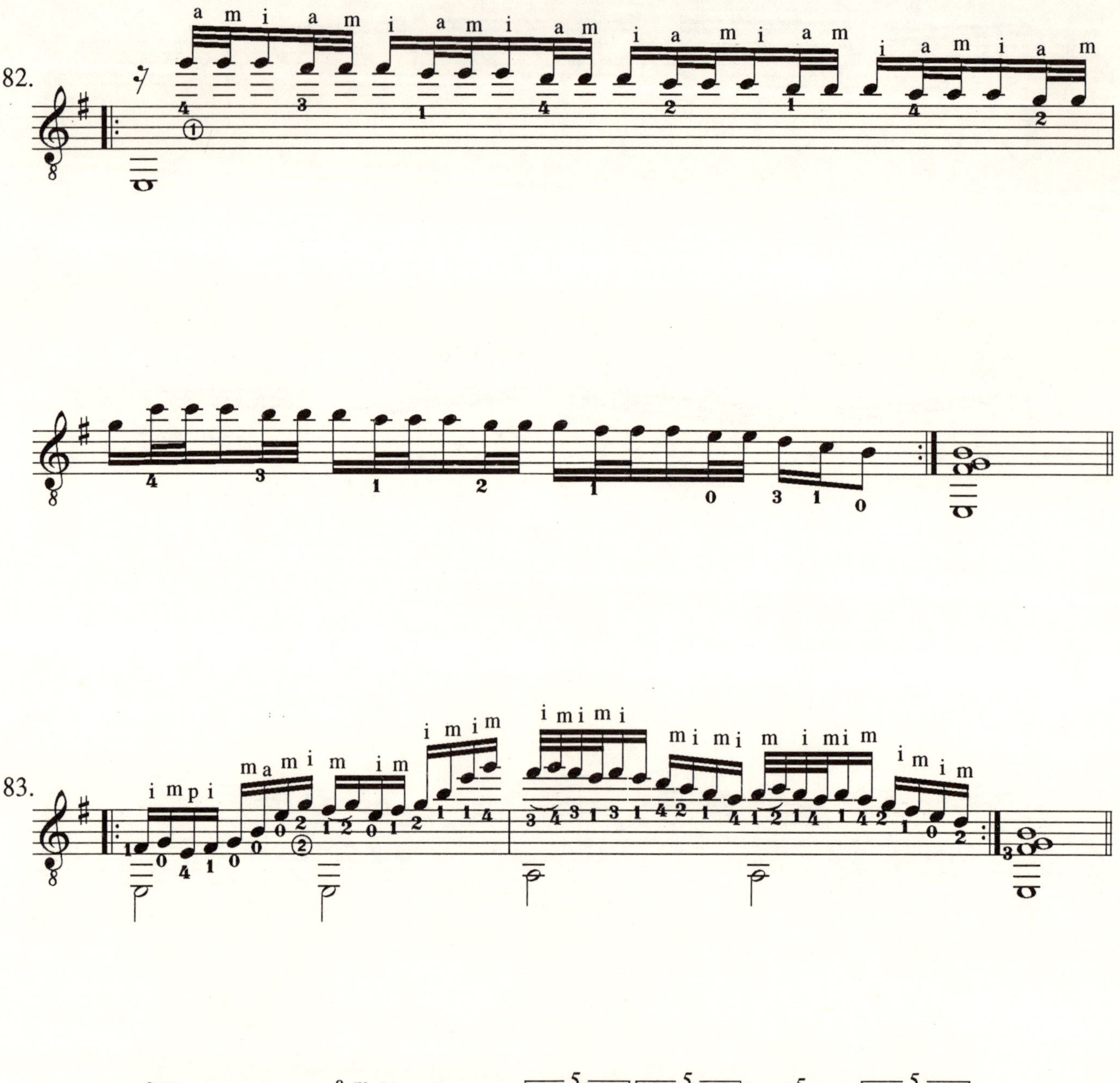
82.
83.
84.
85.

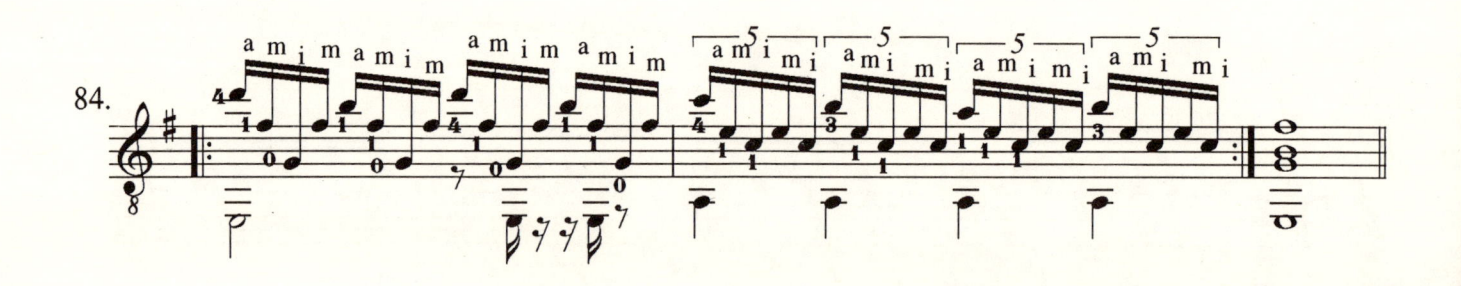

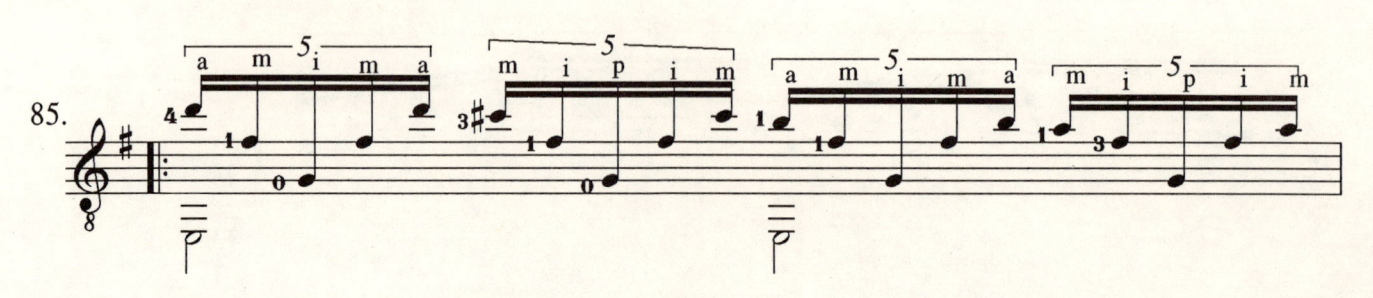

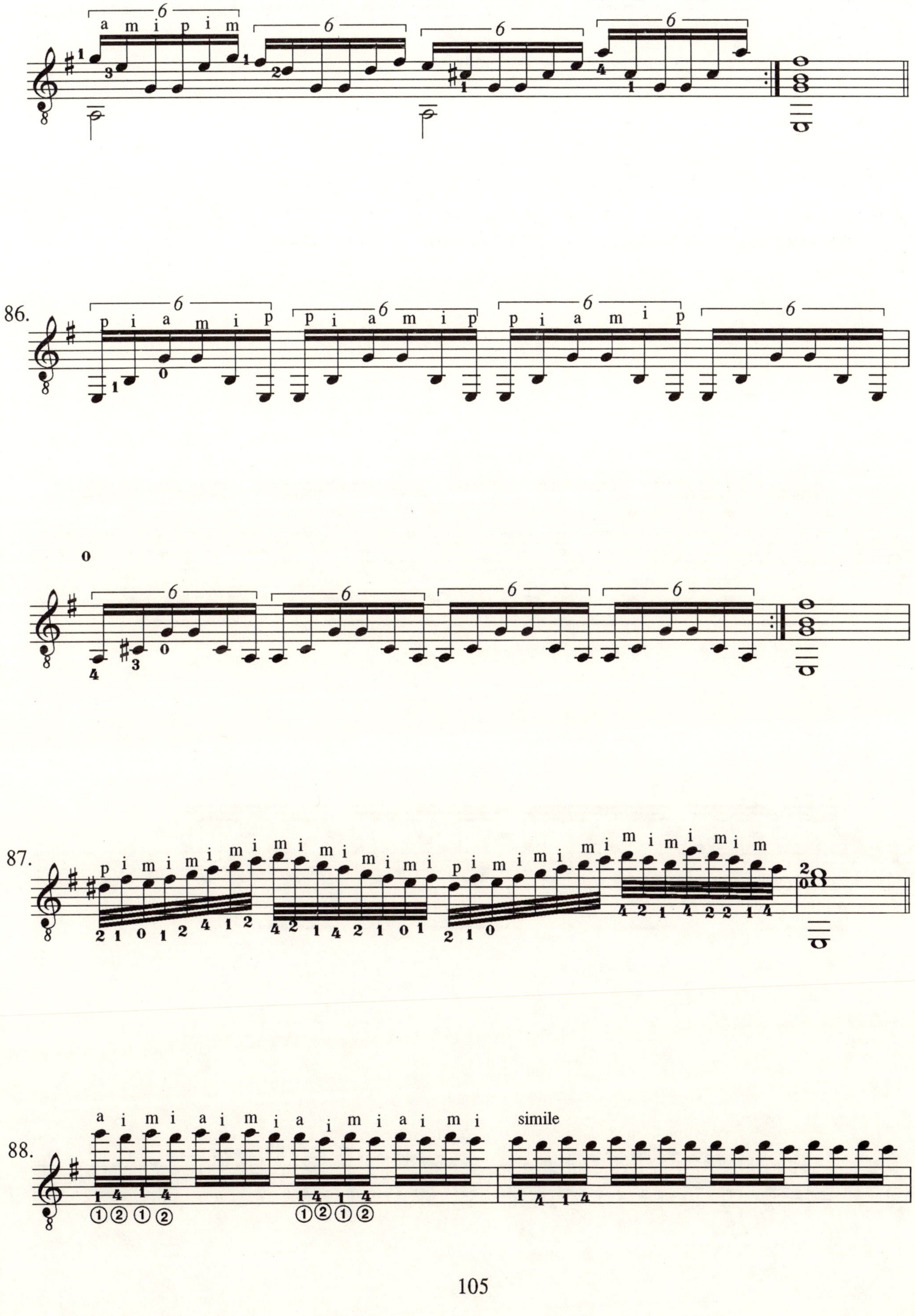
86.
87.
88.
simile

106

107

95.

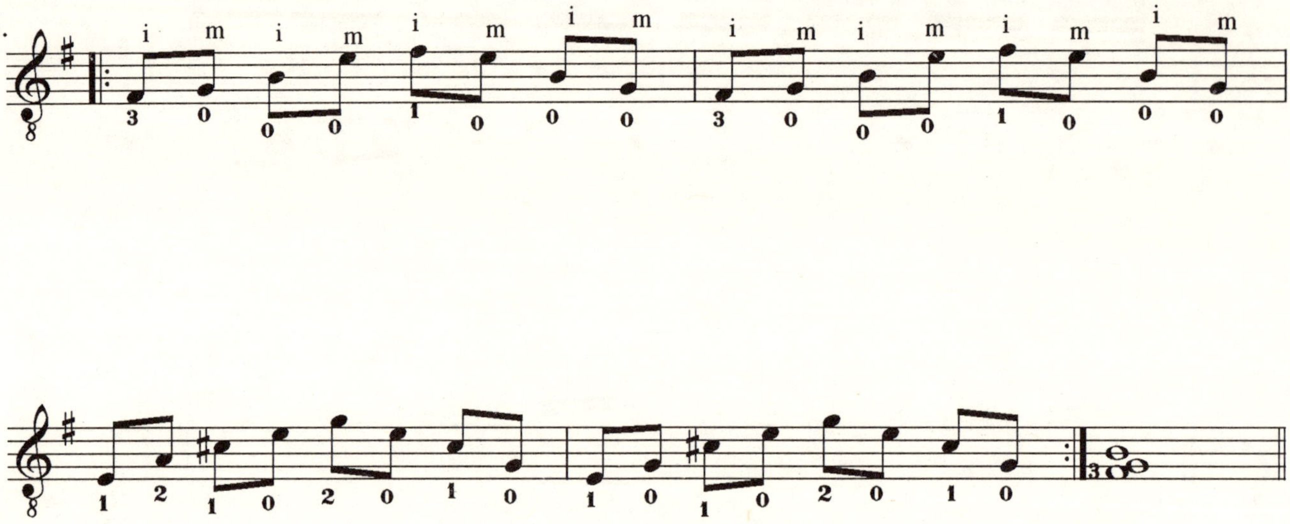

96.

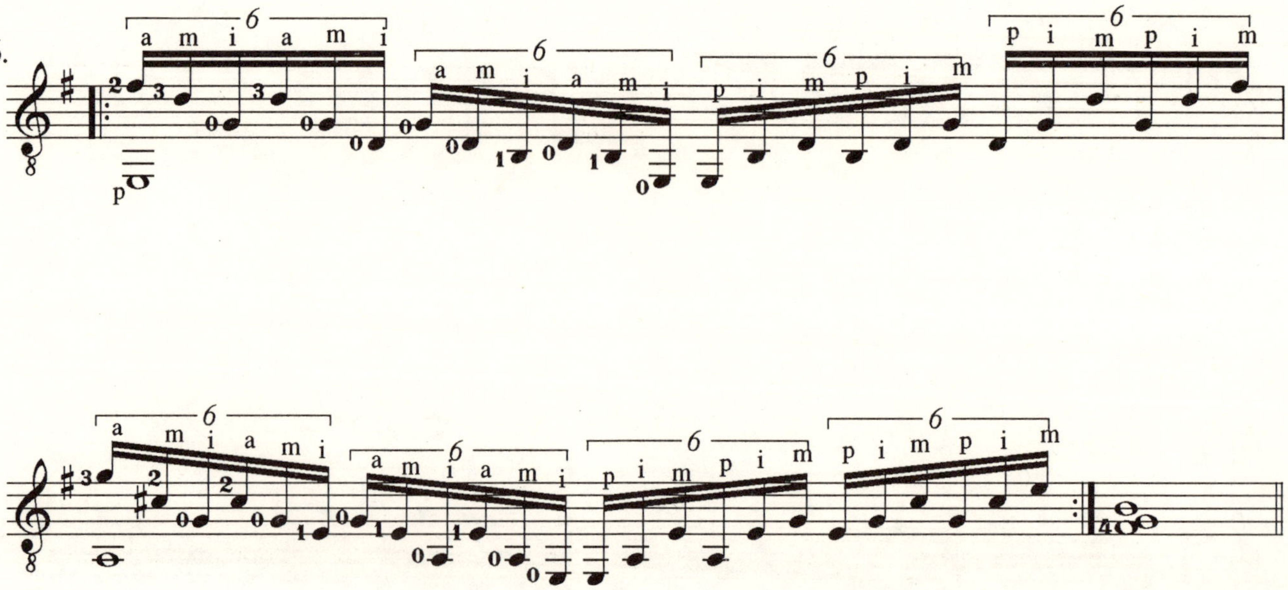

97.

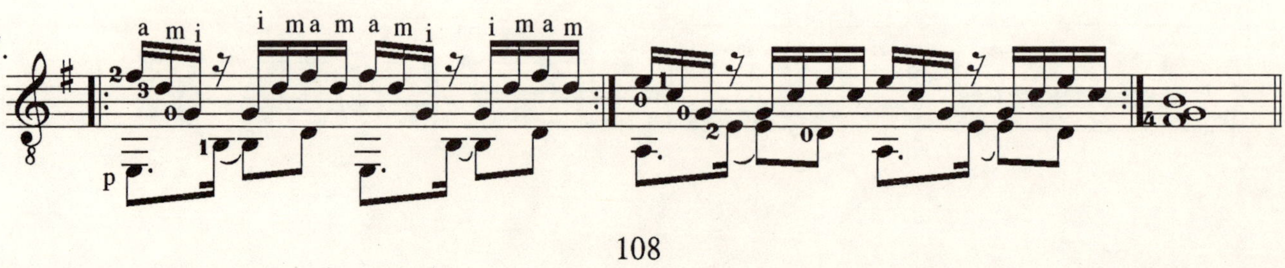

109

Sources

1. John Williams - *Guitar Magazine (U.K) Nov '82*
2. Pepe Romero - *Guitar Style and Technique* - Bradley Publications
3. Andrés Segovia - *Maestro Segovia (Graham Wade)* - Robson Books
4. Fernando Sor - *Method For The Spanish Guitar* - Da Capo Press - New York
5. Andrés Segovia - *Segovia (Graham Wade)* Allison & Busby, London and New York
6. Pepe Romero - *Guitar Style and Technique* - Bradley Publications
7. Yehudi Menuhin - *Unfinished Journey* - Alfred A. Knopf - New York
8. Vincent Van Gogh - *The Letters of Vincent Van Gogh* - Fontana
9. Gerald Moore - *Am I Too Loud?* - Penguin Books
10. Anton Rubinstein - *The World of the Concert Pianist (David Dubal)* Gollancz - London.
11. Andrés Segovia - *Maestro Segovia - (Graham Wade)* - Robson Books
12. Michel de Montaigne - *Essays* - Penguin Classics
13. David Dubal - *The World of the Concert Pianist* - Gollancz - London
14. Leo Brouwer (anecdotal)
15. Dinu Lipatti - *The World of the Concert Pianist* - Gollancz - London
16. Andrés Segovia - *Maestro Segovia - (Graham Wade)* - Robson Books
17. Gary Player - *The Independent - February 5th. 1998*
18. Vladimir de Pachmann - *The World of the Concert Pianist* - David Dubal
19. Andrés Segovia - *Maestro Segovia - Graham Wade* - Robson Books
20. Judi James - *Body Talk*
21. Glenn Gould - *Glenn Gould - The Agony and Ecstasy of Genius* - Peter F. Oswald - W.W. Norton and Co. - New York and London
22. Daniel Barenboim - *Classical Guitar Magazine March '97.*
23. Glenn Gould - *Glenn Gould - The Agony and Ecstasy of Genius* - Peter F. Oswald - W.W. Norton & Co. - New York and London
24. Eric Satie - *Diary of an Amnesiac* - Ernst Eulenberg 1980
25. Pepe Romero - *Guitar Style and Technique* - Bradley Publications
26. Gaspar Sanz - *Instrucción De Musica Sobre La Guitarra Espanola Y Metodo De Sus Primeros Rudimentos Hasta Tanerla Con Destrera.*
27. Celedonio Romero - *The Celedonio Romero Method for the Classical Guitar* - Juan Orozco Corporation P.O.Box 469 Woodmere, New York.
28. Claudio Arrau - *The World of the Concert Pianist* - David Dubal - Gollancz - London
29. Yehudi Menuhin - *Unfinished Journey* - Knopf - London
30. Agustín Barrios - - Richard Stover - Belwyn Mills Music
31. Michel de Montaigne - *Essays* - Penguin Classics
32. Vivekananda - *The Tibetan Book of Living and Dying* - Sogyal Rinpoche - Rider
33. Confucius - *The Tibetan Book of Living and Dying* - Sogyal Rinpoche - Rider